The Gourmet Girls Go Camping

Cookbook

The Gourmet Girls Go Camping
Cookbook

Amazing meals straight from your campfire!

Gail Kearns, Lindsey Moran, and Denise Woolery

Mise en Press
Santa Barbara, California

Published by Mise en Press
825 East Pedregosa Street, Suite 2
Santa Barbara, CA 93103

Library of Congress Control Number: 2016916511

ISBN: 978-0-9975214-1-2

Edited by Gail Kearns

Written and illustrated by Lindsey Moran

Recipes by Denise Woolery and Gail Kearns

Photography by Adam James, Denise Woolery, Lindsey Moran, Arny Cano,
and The Gourmet Girls at Large

Food styling by Denise Woolery

FIRST EDITION

Printed in China through Lorna Johnson Print

"Everybody needs beauty as well as bread, places to play in and pray in, where Nature may heal and cheer and give strength to body and soul alike."
—John Muir, *The Yosemite*, 1912

Contents

Left to right, top row: Gail Kearns, Denise Woolery, Yvonne Chin, Wendy Overend.
Bottom row: Lyn Burich, Maury Treman, and Seyburn Zorthian. Not pictured: Jen Shively and Lindsey Moran.

Introduction

One fine day, as Gourmet Girls Gail and Denise were sitting at their perfectly curated picnic table in Big Sur, enjoying a delicious fire-roasted meal, Gail announced, "I think we should write a cookbook!" It was an excellent idea, and we immediately set about making it happen. Little did we know what it would entail to produce a book unlike any other currently on the market. We did our research and found that there really aren't many camp cookbooks geared to the gourmet palate. Sure, there were plenty of books about glamping and retro trailers, but no one had come up with a cookbook that addressed the gourmet in all of us. After all, who says you have to eat beans and weenies just because you're camping? Boring! Camping is supposed to be fun; you shouldn't be forced to eat prison gruel. As lovers of fresh, well-prepared food, we've been adapting recipes for the campsite for years.

As campers we all know there's nothing better than waking up in the woods to the sound of a babbling brook and birds chirping. Oh wait, yes there is, eating apricot-pecan pancakes with blackberry maple syrup. That's better! In this cookbook we aim to answer the age-old question, why not do both? Reap the benefits from years of experience: every burnt marshmallow, every soggy bit of lettuce, and every forgotten spice. Our soggy mistakes are about to become your culinary triumphs.

The Gourmet Girls began in 1996 in Santa Barbara as a couple of friends getting together for a potluck dinner and quickly grew into a diverse and dynamic group of women

Left to right: Lindsey Moran, Gail Kearns, Seyburn Zorthian, Yvonne Chin, Denise Woolery, Wendy Overend, Jen Shively. Not pictured: Lyn Burich and Maury Treman.

with discerning palates, sharing our culinary adventures. We have come together every year since then for the holidays, our annual gourmet camping trip, and our well-loved summer paella party. At each gathering, we bring mouthwatering dishes to share along with our laughter, our tears, our love of the outdoors and one another, as well as our mutual love of food.

Jen has a popular catering company that provides a delectable bill of fare to residents in the community. Seyburn is part owner of a Santa Ynez Valley winery and an extraordinary fine artist. Gail is a book sherpa who helps writers make the trek from manuscript to getting published. Yvonne, Maury, and Denise design landscapes for the many spectacular homes in and around Santa Barbara. Lyn is a civil engineer and a surfing instructor for our wounded and recovering veterans. Wendy, our PhD from South Africa, is director of admissions at a university, and Lindsey is a film and TV production designer. Together we make up the Gourmet Girls at Large.

Everyone helped develop, test, and taste many of the recipes during our lively get-togethers. Whether you're barbecuing in your backyard or sleeping out under the stars, our favorite camping palate pleasers are a must for all foodies. We hope you'll be as pleased with the results as we are. Okay, we're being modest; these recipes are completely amazing. It's time to make your camp neighbors jealous!

To Gear or Not to Gear

Before you get started, you'll need to know what to bring, and more important, what's okay to leave behind. Your gear is just as important as your ingredients. Once you get to your campsite, there isn't always a Gourmet-Girl-worthy grocery store or a Sur La Table nearby. If you forget a wine opener, it's likely you'll be able to find one at a neighboring campsite. However, if you forget something as important as your paring knife or cutting board, you might find yourself sporking a tomato against a rock. This behavior is unacceptable. Just like Santa before his big day, we recommend making a list and checking it twice.

Pro camp chefs end up with all their necessary items in a special bin dedicated to the sport of Camp Cheffing (we're looking into Olympic recognition). Dedicated bins ensure you'll always have exactly what you need every time. From now on when a sad neighbor camper ends up on your "tentstep," you can let them choose from your fanciful array of wine openers.

Our favorite gear has been carefully curated over the years, and we believe no camping experience is complete without every piece.

❧ Setting Up Camp ❧

» Camp chair
» Tent
» Tarp (spread out under tent)
» Hammer (for those hard-to-teach kids... oh, wait, never mind, this is for tent pegs)
» Sleeping pad or blow-up mattress (rocks be damned)
» Blankets and/or sleeping bag
» Pillow
» Tent light
» Indoor/outdoor rug to use as a front porch (keep that dusty wilderness out of your comfy tent)

» Folding side table
(to hold your morning coffee or your cocktail)
» Hammock
(because let's face it, you don't really want to go on that hike)

⇒ For the Fire ⇐

» Fire poker
» Firepit gloves
» Charcoal
» Charcoal chimney starter
» Long fireplace matches
» Grill brush
» Long metal tongs for moving charcoal

⇒ Cooking Gear ⇐

» Tuscan grill or similar grilling surface
» Dutch oven 12"
» Dutch oven lid lifter—REI or World Market (Lodge)
» Dutch oven tripod—World Market (Lodge)
» Trivet for Dutch oven
» Parchment paper Dutch oven liners
» Cast iron griddle for making pancakes and other fare
» Volcano grill (www.volcanogrills.com)
» Volcano Dutch oven
» Volcano heatproof hood
» Wonderbag (www.wonderbagworld.com)

⇒ Equipment Key ⇐

» (DO) = Dutch Oven
» (CS) = Camp Stove
» (TG) = Tuscan Grill
» (V) = Volcano
» (W) = Wonderbag

⇒ The Camp Kitchen ⇐

» Camp stove
» 1 lb propane cylinders
(2–3 per day, depending on BTUs of stove) or 20 lb propane tank and adapter
» Heat diffuser for camp stove
» Gas lantern and 1 lb propane cylinder (keep an extra on hand)
» Camp kitchen (REI, optional)
» Ice chest cooler

⇒ The Kitchen Sink ⇐

» Headlamp
» Helio pressure shower
(optional: we use this to rinse dishes at our dishwashing station and boy is it a dream)
» Two wash bins for doing dishes
(one for hot water soaking and washing, one for cold water rinsing)
» Dish drying rack
» Dishtowels

❧ Tools of the Trade ❧

» Stainless steel pots and pans
» Pasta pot with colander
» 6" nonstick fry pan for eggs
» Perforated pan for pizza or pizza stone
» Pizza peel, a long-handled board for sliding under pizza
» Shellfish cooking rack
» Fish basket
» Taco rack
» Sharp knives (chef, small ceramic knife)
» Chef's knife roll
» Joyce Chen kitchen shears
» Cutting boards (buy the thin plastic ones that come 3–4 to a package)
» Citrus zester
» Mandoline
» Garlic press
» Sieve
» Measuring cups (dry goods)
» Measuring cup (liquids)
» Measuring spoons
» Whisk
» Spatula
» Ladle
» Wooden spoons
» Bamboo or metal skewers
» Can opener
» Corkscrew
» Stainless steel cocktail shaker
» Coffee maker (options: French press or Melitta cone filters and holder)
» Milk frother
» Camp toaster
» Insulated mug
» Extra batteries for gadgets
» Tablecloth
» Napkins or paper towels
» Large nonbreakable salad bowl
» Large platter
» Mess kit (plate, bowl, cup, flatware)
» Collapsible flower vase
» Apron (you don't want to mess up your awesome forest print leggings!)

Tips and Tricks

≋ Prep It ≋

We'd like to stress the importance of prepping at home. The more you prep at home, the easier your fireside chef experience will be. Everything in the book can be done at the campsite, but preparing things like sauces, chopping vegetables, and doing any other remedial tasks ahead of time will extend your afternoon hike or cocktail hour and save your fire-roasted hands from unnecessary dishwashing.

≋ Check It ≋

Always call ahead and check with your campground to see whether or not campfires are allowed and whether you need to bring your own wood or can buy it on site. If campfires are not allowed, don't despair! You can use a propane-fueled portable firepit to gather around and even cook on. These are available at most RV stores.

≋ Freeze It ≋

For heaven's sake, prechill your cooler! This makes a big difference in how long your food will stay cold. You can also help it along by freezing meats in their marinade before you leave. Pack prefrozen items around fresh ingredients in the cooler to ensure your finely selected vittles don't get wilted and soggy in the swamp that is sure to be your cooler on day three. Do not, under any circumstances, place your salad greens, tomatoes, or fresh herbs next to anything frozen. Keep them up high in the cooler and invest in some heavy-duty freezer bags. Double bag anything susceptible to waterlogging, wilting, or leaking. Dill infused havarti is fantastic, but not if it's also infused with the melted ice water from the dregs of your cooler.

⋐ Store It ⋑

Keep knives inside your firepit mitt or buy a chef's knife case. Use several watertight plastic bins for storing your dedicated camping supplies such as kitchen items, dry goods, and miscellaneous camping equipment.

⋐ Catch It ⋑

Heading to a river or lakeside campground? Make sure you get a fishing license before you leave home. Keep all of your fishing gear together in one place: rod, reel, net, stringer, and bait. Once you catch a fish, dispatch it to the rainbow bridge quickly with a knife blade into the top of the head. While completely horrifying to actually do, this is the most humane way to go about it. Without further adieu, gut it, scale it, and cook it! (see Grilled Trout Wrapped in Bacon, page 98).

⋐ Burn It ⋑

We can't even count how many times we've heard arguments about the proper way to build a fire. Here's our two cents: Bring a bag of fatwood and some fire starters or newspaper to get your fire started. Slowly add small pieces of wood until you have flames. Once you have it going, add one larger log and wait for it to catch fire. Then place another parallel to that one, leaving a gap between them. Next, add two more logs on top of those, perpendicular to the bottom ones, again leaving a gap between them. It will look like a hash tag # (this should be rudimentary for Millennials). As the logs burn down, keep adding two logs perpendicular to the ones below them. Think of it as reposting a hash tag.

⋐ Cook It ⋑

For the Tuscan grill, knock the fire down so that you have a thick bed of glowing coals. Place the grill over the fire ring and let it heat up. When there is a film of white ash on the coals, you are ready to cook.

For the Dutch oven, build your campfire to one side of your firepit. When your fire is going fast and furious, add some charcoal to the center of the fire. Once the coals have a white ash coating, move some of them, using your extra-long metal tongs (don't forget to wear your thick fireproof mitts), to the center of the firepit. Place your cast iron tripod over the firepit, keeping the tripod legs inside the firepit if possible. Hang your Dutch oven from the tripod chain so that it is as close to level and centered as you can get it. Place the coals around the bottom according to the Dutch Oven Coal Placement Chart (right). Adjust the height of the Dutch oven using different chain links attached to the tripod, so the bottom is just above the ring of coals. Adjust the cooking temperature by raising and lowering the oven (this takes practice) or by adding and subtracting the amount of coals on the top and bottom of the oven. To sauté ingredients prior to cooking (such as in our Braised Short Ribs, page 128), keep the oven very close to the coals so that the ingredients sizzle when they hit the inside. Add remaining ingredients and place the lid on the Dutch oven with a cast iron lid lifter, and add coals to the lid according to the chart. Keep adding wood and coals to your fire for the duration of cooking as needed.

⮞ Dutch Oven Coal Placement Chart ⮜

F/C	8" DO Top	8" DO Btm.	10" DO Top	10" DO Btm.	12" DO Top	12" DO Btm.	14" DO Top	14" DO Btm.
325°/160°	10	5	13	6	16	7	20	10
350°/180°	11	5	14	7	17	8	21	11
375°/190°	11	6	16	7	18	9	22	12
400°/200°	12	6	17	8	19	10	24	12
425°/215°	13	6	18	9	21	10	25	13
450°/230°	14	6	19	10	22	11	26	14

⮞ Metric Conversion Chart ⮜

Volume US	Volume Metric	Weight US	Weight Metric	Temp. F	Temp. C
1 teaspoon	5 ml	½ ounce	15 g	250°	120°
1 tablespoon	15 ml	1 ounce	30 g	300°	150°
¼ cup	60 ml	3 ounces	90 g	325°	160°
⅓ cup	75 ml	4 ounces	115 g	350°	180°
½ cup	125 ml	8 ounces	225 g	375°	190°
⅔ cup	150 ml	12 ounces	350 g	400°	200°
¾ cup	175 ml	1 pound	450 g	425°	220°
1 cup	250 ml	2¼ pounds	1 kg	450°	230°

Lovely Libations

Let's face it, the minute you get settled the first thing on most everyone's agenda is a drink. You woke up early, drove five million miles, and meditated your way through multiple episodes of road rage to get to the campground. You've schlepped your multitudinous amounts of gear all the way across the campsite and wrestled your wily tent poles into submission. It's time for a tasty reward. For the kiddos and non-imbibers there are plenty of G-rated drinks and delicious mocktail options as well.

While a true Gourmet Girl never wavers in the face of a Classic Dry Martini (page 30), we don't see any reason you shouldn't jazz it up a little. From standards like The Mighty Manhattan (pictured left, recipe page 36) to some simple camper-friendly apéritifs, the drink recipes in this chapter outline the necessary steps to get your "toasty" on and sip yourself a nice warm sweater before that chilly night sets in.

The most important thing to remember when preparing your afternoon cocktail, don't blow your wad too early. We recommend only a drink or two in the afternoon. Part of the beauty of camping is that since you've abandoned your vehicle in the overflow parking lot for a few days, all the garden gnomes between your favorite watering hole and your house are safe! You'll have plenty of time to work up your tent-threatening stumble during the fantastic dinner and dessert to come.

⇒ Arnold Palmer ⇐

This legacy mocktail gets its title from a professional golfer with the same name.

Serves 1

Ingredients
1 part iced tea
1 part lemonade
Sugar or other sweetener
Lemon, mint, or a slice of kiwi

Directions
Pour equal amounts of iced tea and
lemonade over ice in an 8-ounce glass
and sweeten to taste. Stir and add lemon,
mint, or kiwi as garnish.

Tip: Newman's Own has its own version
of the Arnold Palmer in a portable half-
gallon container. Just add garnish!

⪧ Blackberry Gin Sparkle Farkle ⪦

Make the blackberry honey syrup ahead at home and store it in the fridge in a jar or other container with a tight-fitting lid until ready to transfer to your cooler.

Serves 1

Ingredients
1 ounce blackberry honey syrup (recipe below)
½ ounce lemon juice
1½ ounces Hendrick's Gin
2 ounces soda water
1 lemon wheel and 2 ripe blackberries for garnish

Directions
Pour 1 ounce of prepared honey syrup in the bottom of a collins glass. Add lemon juice and gin and stir. Add ice cubes, then top with the soda water. Garnish with a lemon wheel and a couple of whole blackberries.

Blackberry Honey Syrup

Ingredients
1 cup golden honey
1 cup water
1 package fresh ripe blackberries

Directions
In a medium-sized saucepan, heat the honey and water over medium-low heat. Stir until the honey and water have combined, then remove from the heat. Add the blackberries and muddle them well to incorporate into the honey syrup. When cool, strain through a fine sieve into a jar or other container with a tight-fitting lid.

⮞ Bloody Maryann ⮜

Heated debates regarding the perfect way to mix this classic have landed people searching for water to cool their heated tongues. Spice goes a long way, so remember, everyone's ability to withstand the heat is different. This one's got bite; know your crowd and learn who needs it toned down!

Serves 4

32 ounces veggie juice, shaken
1 cup premium vodka
2 limes, juiced
1 lemon, juiced
2 tablespoons dill pickle juice
1 tablespoon horseradish
2 teaspoons Worcestershire sauce
5 shakes red pepper flakes
4 shakes black pepper or 3 turns ground black pepper
3 shakes cayenne pepper
3 shakes celery salt
1 shake onion powder
½ teaspoon wasabi powder
Crushed salt to taste

Directions
Stir up and serve over ice with a bevy of garnishes.

Suggested garnishes
Sicilian green cracked olives
Pitted purple or black olives
Dill pickles
Pickled green beans

Cherry tomatoes
Pepperoncini
Bacon, cooked

⇒ Camper's Delight ⇐

One of our junior Gourmet Girls stumbled into this fine little recipe while trying to thin her vodka stash. Our (not-so-secret) love of St-Germain can't be understated in this drink.

Serves 1

Ingredients
2 ounces (4 tablespoons) chilled vodka
2 ounces (4 tablespoons) of your favorite juice (we chose Santa Cruz Organic Apricot Mango)
Splash of St-Germain elderflower liqueur
2 lime wedges (one as garnish)
2 ounces (4 tablespoons) sparkling water

Directions
Place vodka, juice, liquor, and juice from one lime wedge into a shaker with ice. Shake that puppy. Strain into a glass. Add sparkling water for a welcome bit of fizz. Garnish with remaining lime wedge and serve.

⇒ Classic Dry Martini ⇐

Contrary to popular belief, a martini does not always need to be shaken. Stirring has always been a perfectly acceptable way to mix the ethanol and juniper in front of you. This makes for a simple way to serve a classic dry martini without too much fussing about.

Serves 1

Ingredients
3 ounces (6 tablespoons) chilled dry gin
1 teaspoon vermouth
3 speared olives or twist of lemon, as a garnish

Directions
Place the vermouth in a shaker with ice. Shake and strain away the excess. Add the gin. Stir and strain into a chilled cocktail glass. Add the olives or lemon twist. Serve.

Tip: You can vary the amount of vermouth, to taste, but the principle remains the same.

⇒ Marvelous Mint Julep ⇐

Serves 1

Ingredients
10 fresh mint leaves, plus a sprig for garnish
1½ teaspoons superfine sugar
Seltzer water
Crushed ice
2½ ounces Kentucky bourbon whiskey

Directions
Place the mint leaves in the bottom of an old-fashioned glass and top with the sugar. Muddle these together until the leaves begin to break down. Add a splash of seltzer water, fill the glass ¾ full with crushed ice, and add the bourbon. Top with another splash of seltzer, stir, and garnish with a sprig of mint. Serve immediately.

⋑ Mom's Own Margarita ⋐

A margarita fit for a kaiju. Packing enough heat to get even the largest Japanese moth monster toasted. Don't drink them too fast or you're likely to get blown off your feet. Invented by veteran camper and executive chef Denise Woolery, we wish you the very best with this little gem of a drink.

Serves 1

Ingredients
2 ounces (4 tablespoons) Hornitos, Cazadores, or similar quality tequila
2 ounces (4 tablespoons) Newman's Own limeade or lemonade
1 ounce (2 tablespoons) Grand Marnier
2 lime wedges
Salt

Directions
Put a decent amount of salt on a plate. Run one lime wedge around the rim of a cup to wet it slightly. Press the rim of the glass firmly down against the salt. Place all ingredients together in a martini shaker with ice. Shake. Strain into the salted cup and serve.

➤ Nojito ➤

This mocktail has all the flavors of the classic Cuban mojito, without the alcohol. Be sure to use fresh mint leaves for the best results! You can make the simple syrup at home and pack it in your cooler when you're ready to head out to the campground.

Serves 1

Ingredients
8 mint leaves
3 ounces lime juice
1½ ounces simple syrup
Crushed ice
2 ounces club soda

Directions
Place mint, lime juice, and simple syrup in an 8-ounce glass.

Lightly mash the leaves together with the liquid using a muddle stick or wooden pestle, being careful not to tear the leaves. You can also use the back of a spoon to release the oils from the mint. Fill the glass with ice, then add club soda. Garnish with mint or a slice of lime, and enjoy!

To make the simple syrup: Place 1 cup water and 1 cup granulated sugar in a container with a tight-fitting lid. Shake vigorously for 3 minutes. Let rest for about 1 minute. Shake again for 30 seconds. Alternatively, you can heat the water and sugar in a small saucepan, stirring until the sugar has dissolved. Cool completely and store, sealed, in your cooler.

⪼ Perfect Paloma ⪻

Serves 1

Ingredients
2 ounces white tequila
½ ounce fresh lime juice
Ice
3 ounces grapefruit soda (Trader Joe's Italian Grapefruit Soda, if available)
Lime slice

Directions
In a highball glass, mix tequila and lime juice. Add ice and top with grapefruit soda. Garnish with lime slice.

⋙ Spiked Hot Cider ⋘

This is a "spiked" version of the traditional hot cider that's great for fall, holiday gatherings, or for warming your hands around the campfire. Make an alcohol-free version for non-imbibers.

Serves 10

Ingredients
6½ cups water
5 orange spice tea bags
1 cup light brown sugar
3½ cups apple cider
2½ cups light rum (optional)
12 cinnamon sticks
2 tablespoons unsalted butter

Directions
Pour water into a large saucepan and bring to a boil. Remove from heat and toss in the orange spice tea bags. Cover and let steep for 5 minutes. Remove tea bags and stir in sugar, apple cider, rum, and 2 of the cinnamon sticks. Heat just to steaming. Do not boil.

Ladle hot cider into mugs and drop ½ teaspoon butter into each.

Garnish with a cinnamon "swizzle" stick.

Tip: Keep extra cider warm in a thermos.

⮞ The Mighty Manhattan ⮜

We've fancied this classic drink up with Luxardo maraschino cherries, trust us, they're worth the extra effort. Find this beauty of a drink pictured on page 24.

Serves 1

Ingredients
Crushed ice
2 ounces whiskey, preferably Bushmills
1 ounce Carpano Antica Formula red vermouth or Cinzano Rosso vermouth
Dash of orange bitters
Maraschino cherries, preferably Luxardo

Directions
Place all ingredients (except cherries) in a cocktail shaker and gently shake. Pour into glasses. Add 2 maraschino cherries and a drop of cherry juice. Stir and enjoy.

⇒ Virgin Mary ⇐

This mocktail is an alcohol-free takeoff on the ever-popular Bloody Mary!

Serves 1

Ingredients
Ice
4 ounces tomato juice
2 teaspoons of freshly squeezed lemon juice, or to taste
½ teaspoon Worcestershire sauce
2 drops Tabasco sauce
Lime wedge

Directions
Fill a large glass with ice. Add tomato juice, then the rest of the ingredients. Stir and garnish with a wedge of lime.

⇒ Gun Butt Coffee ⇐

Just for the hell of it, here's the good, the bad, and the ugly about making cowboy coffee.

Serves 4

Ingredients
Coffee
Water
Fire
Butt of rifle
Half a flask of whiskey (optional)

Directions 1 (the cowboy way)
Bring 1 quart of water to a boil in a saucepan or pot. Grind coffee by crushing whole beans with the butt of a rifle. Watch beans fly in all directions. Add ¾ cup of ground coffee. Return to boil. Immediately remove from heat and cover. Wait until the grounds sink (approximately 5 minutes). They probably won't sink. Serve.

Alternate: Add half a flask of whiskey to help with bitterness.

Directions 2 (the Gourmet Girls way)
Pour 1 quart of water into a pot or saucepan, place the pot on the fire, and bring the water to a boil. Remove from the fire and let sit 30 or 40 seconds.

Add 8 tablespoons of fine grind coffee to the pot and carefully stir the water to get the coffee to mix in. Let the pot sit for 2 minutes, no more. In the end, you should have a total of 4 to 5 minutes brewing time. After 2 minutes, stir the mixture again, re-cover and let sit 2 more minutes. Now pour each cup slowly, trying to leave the coffee grounds in the pot.

Tip 1: Place coffee beans in a dishtowel and pound to a fine grind with a rock. A finer grind of coffee will allow more flavor extraction in less time, and the finer coffee grinds will sink to the bottom easier than more coarse grinds that float more.

Tip 2: Set the pot or saucepan on a mild slope. This way the grounds settle into the corner of the saucepan instead of evenly on the bottom. When you pour the coffee, handle the pot as gently as possible so as not to disturb the grounds. Best to maintain the slope the pan has been sitting at and pour by tilting in that direction. Hold the cup near the pot, move the pot as little as possible.

Tip 3: Sprinkle a palm-full of cool water into the coffee pot. This small amount will not make your coffee cold, but it will help the grounds settle quicker.

Ample Appetizers

What would look nice next to that mocktail or cocktail in your hand? Scallop ceviche with avocado. That's what. Oh, you're not a seafood person (what's wrong with you). Fine. The mushroom crostini, veggie frittata bites, and grilled chicken wings will have to suffice.

Leave the gherkins and weenies at home, please. Some of these power appetizers can be prepped ahead of time at home, so you don't have to worry too much about *cooking* while you're cooking. Since most hors d'oeuvres are finger food by design, there's no course better suited for the woods. We've got a fresh take on wings and a couple of grilled pizza recipes that are sure to become a part of your camping staples.

⋙ Camp-Style Charcuterie Board ⋘

A charcuterie platter is the perfect camping partner!

Adapts to desired number of servings

To create a pleasing looking gourmet charcuterie board, start with the meats: salami, dried sausage, pepperoni, and prosciutto are all good choices. We like to add a flavorful pâté like a duck liver or country-style pâté. Next are the cheeses. One hard cheese and one soft cheese of different shapes add to the presentation. We think a variety of olives as well as dried and fresh fruit are a must. Fruit is seasonal, so make your choices accordingly. Unusual fruits like kiwi, dragon fruit, and persimmons give extra color to a charcuterie board. Additional trimmings could include marinated artichokes, peppers, carrots, and, of course, cornichons.

Have fun arranging your selections, adding any items like jams, nut butters, and mustards. Then grab the bread and crackers and enjoy!

⋟ Chicken Wings Two Ways ⋞
(TG)

Chicken can be marinated one day ahead. Keep chilled.

Serves 4–6

Ingredients

Juice of 2 lemons

4 garlic cloves, pressed

¼ cup fresh oregano, chopped (or thyme)

¼ cup fresh rosemary, chopped

Salt

Freshly ground pepper

½ cup olive oil

2 pounds meaty chicken wings

Directions

Make ahead: Combine lemon, garlic, oregano, rosemary, and oil in a large, resealable bag. Season with salt and pepper. Add chicken wings, seal bag, and turn to coat. Chill at least 1 hour.

At the campsite: Prepare grill for medium-high heat. Remove wings from marinade. Grill, turning occasionally until golden brown and crisp, 7 to 9 minutes per side.
Use extra marinade for brushing on the wings during cooking. Beware of flare-ups.

Tip: Move the wings to indirect heat to finish cooking. The juices should run clear when cut into.

Variation: Make an effortless barbecue sauce by combining ⅔ cup catsup, ½ cup cider vinegar, ¼ cup brown sugar, 2 teaspoons smoked paprika, 1 teaspoon ground cumin, 1 teaspoon salt, and 1 teaspoon freshly cracked pepper. Place ingredients in a small saucepan over medium heat and cook for 5 minutes. Add water to thin. Brush marinade on chicken wings while grilling. Apply liberally.

⇒ Escargots on the Go ⇐
(CS)

This recipe is courtesy of Jamie Gluck, owner of Bell Street Farm in Los Alamos, California. Escargots butter can be made at home ahead of time.

Serves 3–4

Ingredients
Escargots Butter (recipe below)
1 can French escargots, pull-top for convenience (we like the smaller snails, especially the wild ones from France)
1 loaf bread

Make ahead: Escargots Butter
Ingredients
1 pound good quality salted butter, room temperature
1 large bunch of flat leaf parsley
4 large cloves garlic, peeled

Directions
Set butter out on a plate for an hour. Clean, destem parsley, and spin-dry until all water is removed. Place butter and parsley in food processor with peeled garlic cloves and process until the butter mixture is flecked with very small pieces of parsley but *not* before butter turns too green.

Then, using waxed or parchment paper, roll into a long tube of finished garlic butter. This will keep in your freezer or cooler and you can cut off what you need to use at your convenience.

At the campsite: Rinse escargots under cold water and drain well, then pat dry. Place 12 escargots and 8 tablespoons of your escargots butter in a small skillet over medium heat until bubbling and hot. Be cautious. Any water left on the snails will pop when it is in the melted butter. After about 8 minutes they are ready to eat.

Dunk a piece of bread in the butter, then stab a snail right out of the skillet and put it on a piece of bread (bamboo skewers come in handy for this). Allow it to cool off a little before popping it in your mouth.

Tip: The escargots butter makes a fantastic base for linguine with clams and mussels.

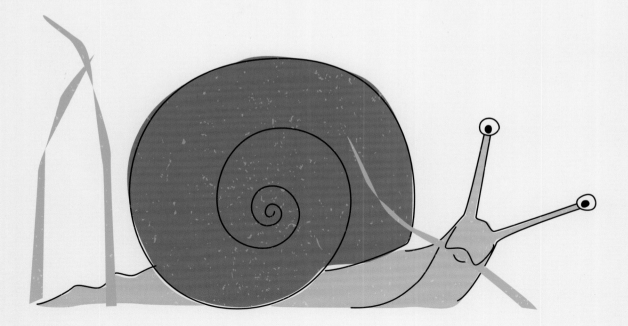

⮞ Grilled Oysters ⮜
(TG)

Serves 3

Ingredients
12 oysters (Pacific or Atlantic)
Fresh parsley, chopped
Lemon wedges
Hot sauce (optional)

Directions
Prepare grill for medium-high heat. Scrub oysters with a stiff brush. Place, cup side down, on shellfish cooking rack (optional) and set on grate. Cover loosely with aluminum foil and grill until oysters begin to open, about 2 minutes. Transfer opened oysters to a platter (discard any that do not open). Let cool slightly, then use a knife to pry shells all the way open. Twist off top shell. Cut muscles connecting oysters to bottom shell. Sprinkle parsley, lemon, and hot sauce, if desired, on top.

Variation: You can make many wonderful sauces for topping oysters: Lemon-Cayenne Vin Blanc (page 195), Lemon Dill Cream Sauce (page 194), and Horseradish Butter (page 192).

≋ Marinated Jumbo Shrimp on the Barbie ≋
(TG or V)

Serves 4

Ingredients
8 jumbo shrimp, shells on
Salt and pepper
1 tablespoon olive oil
1 tablespoon garlic, finely minced
¼ cup lemon juice, freshly squeezed
1½ tablespoons fresh herbs, chopped (whatever you have on hand)

Directions
Use your Joyce Chen kitchen shears to cut the backs of the shrimp through the shell. Remove the vein, using a bamboo skewer. Season shrimp with salt and pepper. In a mixing bowl, combine the olive oil, garlic, lemon juice, and herbs. Add shrimp and allow to marinate for up to 1 hour.

Prepare grill for medium-high heat. Remove shrimp from the marinade. Wipe off excess marinade and place shrimp on the grill. Cook shrimp until they begin to curl and turn pink, about 2 minutes. Turn the shrimp over and cook another 2 to 3 minutes. When grilled to perfection, the shell will come off neatly and cleanly.

Variation: Simply toss shrimp in olive oil and spices or a salt rub before grilling, and serve with your favorite dipping sauce.

➤ Mushrooms Duxelles Crostini ➤
(CS, TG, or V)

Serves 4–6

Ingredients

4 tablespoons butter

4 tablespoons olive oil

1 cup red onion or shallots, finely chopped

3 to 4 garlic cloves, pressed

1 garlic clove, cut in half

5 cups crimini mushrooms, finely chopped

1 tablespoon fresh thyme leaves

Splash of white wine (optional)

3 tablespoons heavy cream

¼ cup Italian parsley

½ teaspoon salt

Freshly ground pepper to taste

1 French baguette (not sourdough)

2 ounces goat cheese

Grated Parmesan cheese

Directions

Sauté red onion or shallots and pressed garlic in 2 tablespoons butter and olive oil for 3 minutes, then add mushrooms. Cook on medium heat until mushrooms release their liquid. Add 1 tablespoon fresh thyme and cook an additional 10 minutes. If using, pour in a splash of white wine. Cook 3 minutes until wine is absorbed. Add heavy cream and parsley. Continue to cook until liquid is absorbed.

Slice ¼-inch rounds of baguette on the bias. Brush with olive oil and grill lightly. Rub top of each baguette round with cut garlic. Smear toasted bread with goat cheese and top with mushroom mixture. Grate a bit of Parmesan over each crostini.

Tip: You can add fresh shiitakes or chanterelles when in season. Dried mushrooms reconstituted are also an option, and add a wonderful smoky flavor.

❧ Mussels and Clams with Garlic, Butter, and White Wine ❧ (TG)

Serves 2

Ingredients
12 fresh mussels or package of frozen mussels (PanaPesca or other)
12 fresh clams or frozen clams (PanaPesca or other)
Garlic, Butter, and White Wine Sauce (page 192)

Directions
Heat grill to medium. Clean mussels and clams if using fresh.

Place clams and mussels on aluminum foil and place on the grill. Cover loosely with another piece of aluminum foil and let steam 10 to 15 minutes, until shells are fully open.

Put shellfish on a platter. Pour garlic sauce over.

Tip: Add mussels and clams with garlic, butter, and white wine sauce to hot cooked pasta for an instant main course.

Variation: Dot each clam and mussel with Cilantro Pesto (page 190).

⇌ PanaPesca Scallops on the Half Shell with Béarnaise Butter ⇌
(TG)

We were over the moon when we discovered PanaPesca seafood products. Here's a delightful appetizer, sure to be a crowd pleaser. Béarnaise butter may be made 5 days ahead and kept chilled, wrapped tightly, until it's ready to be transferred to your cooler.

Serves 6–8

Ingredients
2 PanaPesca packages of Scallops on the Half Shell, frozen
Béarnaise Butter (page 188)

Directions
Prepare grill for medium-high heat. Place a small dollop of Béarnaise butter on each scallop. When coals are ready, carefully place scallops on the half shell directly on the grill. Allow butter to melt, about 5 minutes, and scallops are just cooked. Serve immediately!

Tip: Place frozen scallops in your ice chest and prepare on the first night of your camping trip. Easy preparation and the presentation is truly gourmet!

⧞ Scallop Ceviche with Avocado ⧞

Serves 4

Ingredients
4 large fresh sea scallops, diced
2 tablespoons lime juice, freshly squeezed
¼ teaspoon lime zest
1½ teaspoons balsamic vinegar
1 Hass avocado
2 teaspoons jalapeño, minced (adjust as desired)
2 tablespoons red and orange bell peppers, finely diced
2 tablespoons chives, thinly sliced
3 teaspoons cilantro, thinly sliced
½ teaspoon salt
Freshly ground pepper
1½ tablespoons extra virgin olive oil
Tortilla chips for serving

Directions
Remove muscle from the scallops. Place all ingredients except avocado, cilantro, salt, and peppers in a mixing bowl and toss gently to combine.

Cover and let marinate in the coldest part of cooler for at least 1 hour.

Cut avocado into ½-inch pieces. Just before serving, add avocado, peppers, and cilantro to ceviche.

Season with salt and freshly ground pepper.

Tip: You can substitute 2 cups of bay scallops for sea scallops, and you'll still end up with a delicious ceviche!

⋑ Veggie Frittata Bites ⋐
(CS)

Serves 4

Ingredients
1 tablespoon olive oil
½ sweet onion, chopped
6 green or black olives, chopped
2 whole jarred roasted red peppers, thinly sliced
1 cup baby spinach leaves
8 eggs, beaten
Salt and pepper to taste
¼ cup crumbled feta cheese

Directions
Heat olive oil in a 10-inch nonstick skillet over medium heat on camp stove. Cook onion about 3 minutes. Stir in olives and roasted red peppers and cook for 2 minutes. Add spinach and stir to cook for 1 minute. Whisk salt and pepper into slightly beaten eggs and pour over vegetable mixture. Sprinkle feta cheese over egg mixture. Place a cover on the skillet and reduce heat to medium low. Cook until egg is slightly browned on the bottom, about 3 minutes. Carefully flip the frittata and let brown, about 1 to 2 minutes more. Slide the frittata out of the skillet onto a cutting board. Cut into 8 wedges.

⋗ Salami and Smoked Gouda Pizza ⋖
(TG)

You will need a small pizza stone, a pizza peel, and a small round lid (a wok lid or small Weber BBQ lid works) for the best results, or a round, perforated pan with a handle. Make the Homemade Pizza Dough (page 58) ahead and freeze before your camping trip!

Serves 4

Ingredients

1 premade store bought or Homemade Pizza Dough (page 58)

Olive oil

Garlic, chopped fine

Fresh basil and thyme

1 leek, or 3 green onions, chopped

¼ cup smoked Gouda cheese, grated

6 slices salami or prosciutto

2 small Roma tomatoes, sliced

Semolina flour (for dusting pizza peel)

Directions

When using homemade dough, roll out pizza dough into a 10-inch round or form with hands. Sprinkle flour on pizza peel. Put rolled-out dough on top of peel before adding toppings. For both homemade and premade, brush dough with olive oil and sprinkle with garlic.

Spread leek or green onions and fresh basil on top, then add cheese. Top it off with salami slices, Roma tomatoes, and thyme. Cover with foil or a lid (see note above) and cook over the Tuscan grill on a preheated pizza stone or a pizza pan with small holes. It should take about 15 minutes to get the desired crust over a medium-hot fire. Pizza is done when cheese is melted and crust is golden brown on the bottom.

Tip: Premade pizza crust is a great timesaver when you want homemade pizza but do not have the time to knead the dough and wait for it to rise. Trader Joe's offers both regular and whole wheat crust options. Other brands include Pillsbury, Mama Mary's, and Roma Thin Crust.

⥤ Vegetarian Pizza ⥢
(TG)

You will need a small pizza stone, a pizza peel, and a small round lid (a wok lid or small Weber BBQ lid works!) for the best results, or a round, perforated pan with a handle. Make the Homemade Pizza Dough (page 58) ahead and freeze before your camping trip!

Serves 4

Ingredients
1 premade store bought or Homemade Pizza Dough (page 58)
Olive oil
Garlic, finely chopped
Fresh basil and thyme
1 leek, sliced into thin rounds, or green onions, chopped
6 slices smoked Provolone cheese
1 Japanese eggplant, thinly sliced
2 small Roma tomatoes, sliced
¼ cup goat cheese, crumbled
Semolina flour (for dusting pizza peel)

Directions
When using homemade dough, roll out pizza dough into a 10-inch round or form with hands. Sprinkle flour on pizza peel. Put rolled-out dough on top of peel before adding toppings. For both homemade and premade, brush dough with olive oil and sprinkle with garlic.

Spread leek or green onions and fresh basil on top, then add cheese. Top it off with eggplant slices, Roma tomatoes, and thyme. Dot top of pizza with goat cheese. Cover with foil or a lid (see note above), and cook over the Tuscan grill on a pizza stone or a pizza pan with small holes. It should take about 15 minutes to get the desired crust over a medium-hot fire. Pizza is done when cheese is melted and crust is golden brown on the bottom.

➳ Wild Mushroom Pizza with Caramelized Onions ➵
(TG)

You will need a small pizza stone, a pizza peel, and a small round lid (a wok lid or small Weber BBQ lid works!) for the best results, or a round, perforated pan with a handle. Make the Homemade Pizza Dough (page 58) ahead and freeze before your camping trip!

Makes 2 8-inch pizzas

Ingredients
2 premade store bought or Homemade Pizza Dough (page 58)
7 tablespoons butter, divided
2 tablespoons plus 1 teaspoon olive oil
3 onions, halved lengthwise, thinly sliced crosswise (about 6 cups)
2 pounds assorted wild mushrooms (such as crimini, oyster, chanterelle, and shiitake), cut into bite-size pieces
6 garlic cloves, minced
2 tablespoons minced shallot (about 1 medium)
2 cups dry white wine
1 tablespoon fresh rosemary, minced
3 cups fontina cheese, grated (about 10 ounces)
Semolina flour (for dusting pizza peel)

Directions
Melt 3 tablespoons butter with 2 tablespoons olive oil in a cast iron skillet over medium heat. Add onions and sauté until caramelized, about 45 minutes. Season with salt and pepper.

Melt remaining 4 tablespoons of butter with 1 teaspoon olive oil in another skillet over medium-high heat. Add mushrooms, garlic, and shallot. Sauté 4 minutes. Add wine and simmer until almost all liquid is absorbed, stirring frequently, about 13 minutes. Add rosemary and season with salt and pepper.

Prepare a fire and place Tuscan grill over hot coals. Place pizza stone on top of Tuscan grill and prewarm, unless you are using a round, perforated pan.

When using homemade dough, roll out 2 dough disks on lightly floured surface to 8-inch rounds, allowing dough to rest a few minutes until it springs back. Sprinkle semolina flour on pizza peel, then put rolled-out dough, one at a time, on top of peel before adding toppings.

For both homemade and premade, lightly brush each 8-inch round of dough with olive oil, and then sprinkle with ½ cup of fontina cheese. Scatter 2½ cups of onions over cheese. Scatter ½ cup mushrooms over onions. Sprinkle with salt.

Using the pizza peel, place pizza onto hot pizza stone or transfer to perforated pan.

Place lid over top of pizza and cook for 6 minutes. Lift lid and rotate pizza half a turn. Replace lid and cook until crust is deep brown and top is bubbly, about 6 minutes longer. Check bottom of crust frequently to keep from burning. Let pizza rest for 1 minute, then slice into wedges and serve.

➤ Homemade Pizza Dough ⥎

Make this recipe ahead and freeze dough balls before transferring to cooler.

Serves 4 (Makes about 1½ pounds dough)

The following recipe makes a thin, golden, California-style pizza crust. Parmesan cheese mixed into the dough adds flavor, and olive oil contributes to its crispness.

Ingredients
1 packet (or 1 tablespoon) active dry yeast
2 teaspoons sugar
1½ cups lukewarm water
3 cups all-purpose flour
3 tablespoons Parmesan cheese, grated
1 teaspoon salt
2 tablespoons olive oil

Directions
In a small bowl, dissolve the yeast and 1 teaspoon of the sugar in ½ cup of the lukewarm water. Let it sit until it just begins to foam, 3 to 5 minutes.

To make in a food processor: Put the flour, Parmesan, salt, and remaining sugar in a food processor fitted with the metal blade. Turning the machine on and off rapidly, pulse several times to blend them. With the machine running, pour in the yeast mixture and oil through the feed tube. Then gradually add enough of the remaining water to form a smooth dough. Continue processing until the dough forms a ball that rides around the work bowl on the blade; the dough at this point will be sufficiently kneaded.

To make dough by hand: Stir together the dry ingredients in a large bowl and make a well in the center. Add the liquid ingredients and gradually stir from the center outward. When the ingredients are well combined, remove the dough from the bowl and knead it vigorously on a floured work surface for 5 to 7 minutes, or until it is smooth and elastic.

Transfer the dough to a large bowl that has been coated in olive oil. Cover the bowl with a damp kitchen towel and let the dough rise for 30 to 45 minutes or until it has doubled in bulk. If it is more convenient, you can let the dough rise in the refrigerator for several hours.

Remove the dough from the bowl and cut it in half for a medium-size pizza or in four equal portions for small individual pizzas. The dough is ready to shape and bake.

To freeze the dough, wrap each ball securely in plastic wrap and place in the freezer. The dough will keep well for several weeks. Defrost it at room temperature for 2 to 3 hours before making the pizzas.

Good Morning Eats

If you've curated last night's buzz as well as your nail polish drawer, you'll be ready to start the day out with a new round of gourmet meals. Hopefully you've cleaned up your campsite properly (see "The Neurotic Woodsman," page 209) so there shouldn't be any sign of vermin having had their way with your dinner droppings. Time to light an early fire (see "Tips and Tricks," page 21) to warm your bones and enjoy a hot cup of coffee.

Pancakes are a classic camp-friendly recipe; jazz them up a bit with apricots and pecans. And who said you can't enjoy eggs Benedict in the woods? I'll never forget the day when one of our favorite camp hosts at Ventana Campground in Big Sur joined us to test a couple of recipes and said, "I don't think you guys realize that you're camping!" The irony is, we do, we so do. We simply find no reason to subsist on plain oatmeal and cold cereal for days on end. A true Gourmet Girl can't help but do it any other way.

⥾ Apricot-Pecan Pancakes with Maple-Blackberry Syrup ⥿
(CS or TG)

Serves 10–12 (4-inch diameter pancakes)

Ingredients
2 cups buttermilk pancake mix (We like buttermilk oatmeal pancake mix.)
1½ cups milk
2 eggs
½ teaspoon vanilla extract
½ cup dried apricots, chopped small
½ cup pecan pieces, chopped small
Canola oil or butter

Directions
In a bowl, whisk together the pancake mix, milk, eggs, and vanilla. Stir in dried apricots and pecans. Let batter stand for 4 to 5 minutes.

Heat a cast iron skillet on your camp stove. Coat with 1½ teaspoons canola oil or butter. For each pancake, pour ¼ cup batter and spread with back of a spoon until 4 inches in diameter. Cook until bubbles stop forming on surface or bottom is golden brown. Flip, and cook 1 to 2 minutes or until golden brown. Serve immediately with syrup and extra blackberries.

Maple-Blackberry Syrup

Ingredients
1 pint blackberries, plus several more for garnish
2 cups maple syrup

Directions
Heat syrup and blackberries in a small sauce, macerating blackberries as it heats. Cook for

5 minutes over medium-low flame on camp stove. Strain syrup through a fine sieve into a measuring cup or other vessel with a pourable spout. Drizzle over pancakes or serve on the side. Garnish top of pancake stack with 3 fresh blackberries.

Tip: You can cook these pancakes over your morning fire by waiting until you have a good coal bed, then placing your Tuscan grill over the fire topped with a cast iron griddle. Use the smooth side of the griddle brushed with the oil or butter. You can make many more pancakes at one time using this method. Hungry campers don't like to wait!

⇒ Basque Frittata ⇐
(CS)

Cooking the potatoes can be done ahead of time, but leave them whole until you are ready to add them to the eggs.

Serves 8–10

Ingredients
10 large eggs, beaten
Pinch cayenne
4 cups cold water
Kosher salt
2 tablespoons olive oil
¼ pound fingerling potatoes (about 4 potatoes)
⅓ cup onion, sliced very thin
⅓ cup red bell pepper, julienned
1 tablespoon garlic, minced
¼ pound cured (dry) chorizo, cut into ¼-inch coins
Grated cheddar or crumbled goat cheese
About 5 grinds white pepper from a mill
Salt, to taste
Fresh parsley, chopped
Extra virgin olive oil

Directions
Stir the cayenne into the eggs and set aside.

Put the potatoes and water into a heavy bottomed, 2-quart pot. Add 1 tablespoon kosher salt and bring to a boil over high heat. Lower the heat and cook the potatoes at a simmer until a fork pierces easily to the center of a potato, approximately 20 minutes. Drain in a colander and when cool enough to handle, cut crosswise into ¼-inch thick slices. Set aside.

Put the olive oil in a 10-inch nonstick sauté pan and heat it over medium-low heat. Add the onion, red pepper, and garlic and cook until the vegetables begin to soften, 4 to 5 minutes. Add the chorizo and potatoes and gently stir. Add the eggs, stirring and scrambling them.

Cook until they begin to set up, approximately 4 minutes. Top the eggs with cheese, and then put a lid on the pan. Turn the heat down to low and let cook until the eggs turn nicely golden and cheese is melted, approximately 7 minutes. Place frittata on a large plate.

Season with salt and white pepper, sprinkle with chopped parsley, and drizzle with extra virgin olive oil.

Tip: Frittatas are a great way to use leftovers in your cooler. Chop what's at hand and add them to the egg mixture.

Variation: This would also be delicious with diced tomato and zucchini in the summer or sautéed wild mushrooms in the fall. You can also replace the chorizo with diced bacon.

⇒ Eggs Benedict with Blender Hollandaise ⇐
(CS)

It turns out ex-husbands are good for something! We picked up a simple and delicious way to make a Blender Hollandaise (page 189) that works great on the go.

Serves 4

Ingredients
Butter for coating pan
Water
1 tablespoon white vinegar
8 organic eggs

8 slices Canadian bacon
8 English muffin halves, toasted over the grill
5 fresh chives, snipped

Directions

Make ahead: Blender Hollandaise (page 189). Refrigerate until ready to transfer to your cooler.

At the campsite: To poach eggs, butter the bottom of an 8-inch pan about 2 to 3 inches deep. Fill two-thirds of pan with water, add vinegar, and boil. Turn down heat until water is just below boiling point. Crack eggs one at a time into a small bowl, and carefully slide egg into water. (You can probably fit 4 at a time into pan.) Do not stir or disturb water. Cook to desired doneness, about 6 minutes for a medium-soft yolk. Slide a spatula carefully under each egg to make sure it releases from the bottom of the pan. When ready to serve, remove egg with a slotted spoon.

Meanwhile, reheat hollandaise very slowly in a small saucepan over low heat, being careful not to overheat. If the sauce separates, mix in 1 teaspoon of warm water (from the pan being used to cook the eggs) and whisk. The sauce should come back together. Remove from heat and keep warm until ready to use.

Warm Canadian bacon in a nonstick frying pan on camp stove, 1 minute, being careful not to overcook.

Place 2 toasted, buttered English muffin halves on a plate, top with Canadian bacon, then with a slotted spoon, remove poached egg from water, draining off all water. Place egg on top of bacon, then top with 2 tablespoons (or to taste) hollandaise per muffin half. Repeat with remaining ingredients. Sprinkle each with snipped chives.

Variation: For a vegetarian option, use a slice of Havarti cheese instead of Canadian bacon. Add sliced fresh tomatoes, avocado, and cilantro on top of English muffin half and top with hollandaise. Or use leftover salmon from Campfire Salmon with Lemon Dill Cream Sauce (page 96) instead of Canadian bacon. Delicious!

⇒ Eggs Bruschetta ⇐
(CS)

Serves 2

Ingredients
5 eggs, for scramble
1 tablespoon chives, snipped
1 tablespoon butter
1 ciabatta, sliced lengthwise
1 garlic clove, halved widthwise
½ avocado, sliced
8 yellow and red cherry tomatoes, halved
Fistful of fresh basil, chopped
Olive oil

Directions
Whisk eggs in a bowl. Add chives. Put butter in a medium fry pan and scramble eggs. Meanwhile toast ciabatta in a pan or on a camp toaster. Rub with garlic half and drizzle with olive oil. Mash avocado onto one side of ciabatta. Pile on scrambled eggs and top with cherry tomatoes and basil. Drizzle on a little more olive oil. Salt and pepper to taste.

⋙ Individual French Omelets ⋘
(CS)

Serves 2

Ingredients
2 tablespoons butter
4 eggs, whisked
Salt and pepper
Cheese of your choice
Fresh herbs

For the filling: You can use anything you want inside of these omelets. A classic French version is diced ham, chopped fresh parsley and chives, and about 1 tablespoon grated Gruyère cheese.

Other options: Fresh chopped tomatoes, avocado, and cilantro with grated Parmesan.

Directions
Whisk 2 eggs at a time in a bowl. Heat butter in a small 7-inch nonstick frying pan. When butter is bubbling, pour in eggs and quickly tip pan in all directions in a circular motion to spread egg mixture evenly over the bottom of the pan. Drag eggs in from the side of the pan where egg is mostly cooked and tip pan so that raw egg in the center flows to the edges of the pan. Maintain a round shape with the eggs.

Place filling ingredients in the center of the setting egg mixture from top to bottom in a narrow column, and carefully fold both sides inwards, one over the other until you have a cylinder. Carefully flip omelet over, seam side down in pan, and cook until there is no more raw egg seeping from the ends. Repeat with remaining ingredients to make second omelet. Remove from pan and serve with your favorite garnish.

⮑ Peach and Lemon Mascarpone French Toast ⮐
(CS or TG)

You can easily cook the peaches ahead of time at home, saving time at the campsite.

Serves 4

Ingredients
4 tablespoons unsalted butter
2 tablespoons light brown sugar
2 ripe yellow peaches, cut into ½-inch pieces
¾ cup mascarpone
1 teaspoon vanilla extract
Zest of 2 lemons
1 teaspoon lemon juice
8 slices white bread or brioche, preferably day old
6 large eggs
1 cup heavy cream
⅛ teaspoon nutmeg
⅛ teaspoon ground cinnamon
Confectioner's sugar

Directions

Make ahead: In a large skillet, over medium-low heat, melt 2 tablespoons of the butter until it foams. Add the brown sugar and stir for 30 seconds. Add the peaches, raise heat to medium-high, and cook, stirring frequently, for 3 minutes. Transfer to a container and refrigerate until ready to transfer to cooler.

At the campsite: In a small bowl, combine the mascarpone, vanilla, lemon zest, and juice. Stir until smooth.

Place 4 slices of the bread on a cutting board. Spread mascarpone mixture evenly on all 4 slices of bread. Divide the peach mixture evenly among the slices, leaving a ½-inch border on all sides. Top with another slice of bread and press gently.

In a shallow bowl, beat the eggs, cream, nutmeg, and cinnamon. Working in batches, soak the sandwiches in the egg mixture for 5 minutes per side.

Melt 1 tablespoon of the butter in a large skillet or use a cast iron griddle over two burners on your camp stove. Fry 2 sandwiches over medium heat until golden brown, 3 to 4 minutes per side. Sprinkle with confectioner's sugar. Serve immediately.

Tip: You can cook these over your morning fire too! Just wait until you have a nice coal bed, then break the fire down a bit, place your Tuscan grill over the fire, and top it with a cast iron griddle. We have one that has one ribbed side and one smooth side. For the French toast use the smooth side. Add the butter to the griddle once it has warmed up and cook as directed above. Yum!

Variation: Use raspberry jam and lemon curd on top of the mascarpone instead of peaches.

⊱ Quinoa Breakfast Bowl ⊰
(CS)

Ideal for morning fare. Make it instead of oatmeal.

Serves 1–2

Ingredients
½ to 1 cup leftover plain cooked quinoa
¼ to ½ cup vanilla nondairy milk (almond or hemp milk are good)
1 teaspoon maple syrup
Cinnamon, nutmeg, and/or cardamom, to taste
½ cup fresh fruit of your choice (diced apple, pear, mango, sliced banana, whole blueberries or raspberries, sliced strawberries)
A sprinkling of nuts and/or seeds (choose from chopped walnuts or pecans, sliced almonds, pistachios, pumpkin seeds, sunflower seeds, hemp, or chia seeds)

Directions
Warm the cooked quinoa in a small saucepan with nondairy milk.

When most of the nondairy milk has been absorbed, transfer to a bowl. Stir in maple syrup and spice, to taste.

Top with fruit, nuts, and seeds. Serve at once.

Tip: Cook a fair amount of quinoa before your camping trip. It's a superfood you can use to bulk up a salad, or give it the oatmeal treatment like we've done here.

Quinoa Breakfast Skillet
(CS)

Serves 4

Ingredients
4 slices thick-cut bacon, chopped
1 small sweet potato, chopped
½ red onion, chopped
½ red pepper, chopped
½ green pepper, chopped (optional)
1 cup sliced mushrooms, chopped
2 garlic cloves, minced
½ cup uncooked quinoa, rinsed
1 cup low-sodium vegetable or chicken stock (or water)
4 eggs, cooked your desired way
Salt and pepper to taste

Directions
Heat a large skillet over medium heat and add bacon. Cook until fat is rendered and bacon is crispy, then remove bacon with a slotted spoon and place on a paper towel to drain. Reduce heat to medium-low and add sweet potato, onions, peppers, mushrooms, and garlic to the skillet, tossing to coat. Cover and cook for 5 to 6 minutes, stirring once or twice, until soft. Add uncooked quinoa to vegetables and stir for 1 to 2 minutes, allowing it to lightly toast. Pour in stock or water and bring the mixture to a boil. Immediately reduce to a simmer, cover and cook for 15 minutes or until quinoa is cooked through. While quinoa is cooking, prepare eggs. Once cooked, taste and season to your liking. Serve quinoa in bowls topped with eggs and cooked bacon.

⮞ Super Easy Campfire Breakfast Burritos ⮜
(CS, TG)

A portion of this recipe is a make-ahead, saving you time and getting you on the hiking trails earlier in the day. We think it's always good to beat the crowds!

Serves 4

Ingredients
4 russet or Yukon Gold potatoes, peeled, chopped, and parboiled until just tender
4 tablespoons green onions, sliced
¼ cup cilantro, chopped
6 breakfast sausage, browned and crumbled, or 1 cup cooked ham, diced
8 eggs, beaten (about 2 per burrito)
Heavy duty foil
4 large tortillas, flour or whole wheat
1 can refried beans (optional)
Cheddar cheese, grated
Salt and pepper
Salsa or hot sauce for serving (optional)

Directions

Make ahead: Season parboiled potatoes with salt and pepper. Add sliced green onions and cilantro to potatoes and stir to combine. Add browned breakfast sausage (or ham) and put into a plastic resealable bag or portable container. Refrigerate until ready to pack cooler. Store in cooler until ready to make burritos.

At the campsite: Prepare a fire for medium-hot coals. When coals are ready, warm a frying pan on your cook stove. Add the potato/sausage mixture to the hot pan, stirring often, until potatoes begin to brown and mixture is heated through. Add beaten eggs to potato mixture and cook until eggs are scrambled.

Meanwhile, lay out large squares of foil, each with a tortilla on top. If using refried beans, spread a thin layer of refried beans onto the middle of each tortilla. Top with potato/sausage/egg mixture. Sprinkle cheese on top of that.

Fold burrito, then roll each one up in foil and place over the campfire. Cook burritos, flipping once, about 5 minutes per side (depending on the heat of your campfire) or until cheese is melted and burrito is heated completely through (the tortillas will get some browning and charring on them, which is good). Just watch carefully that you don't burn them.

⋙ Toasted Coconut Pancakes ⋘
(CS or TG)

Serves 10–12 (4-inch diameter pancakes)

Ingredients
½ cup shredded unsweetened coconut
1 cup whole wheat flour
1 teaspoon baking powder
½ teaspoon each salt and cinnamon
¼ teaspoon nutmeg
⅛ teaspoon baking soda
¾ cup light coconut milk
½ cup warm water
1½ tablespoons honey
2 teaspoons pure vanilla extract

Directions
Toast coconut in a medium pan over medium heat on the camp stove, shaking pan frequently, until golden brown, 2 to 3 minutes. Cool and set aside.

In a bowl, whisk together whole wheat flour, baking powder, salt and cinnamon, nutmeg, and baking soda.

In another bowl, whisk together the coconut milk, water, honey, and vanilla. Stir into dry ingredients along with the toasted coconut to form a thin batter.

Heat a skillet with 1½ teaspoons butter or vegetable oil. For each pancake, pour ¼ cup batter and spread with back of a spoon until 4 inches in diameter. Cook until bubbles form, 2 to 3 minutes. Flip and cook 1 to 2 minutes. Serve immediately with syrup and relish.

Ginger-Lime Syrup

Ingredients
1 cup agave syrup
1 tablespoon fresh ginger root, minced
1 tablespoon lime juice, freshly squeezed
Zest of one lime

Directions
Heat agave syrup in a small saucepan. Add ginger, lime juice, and zest. Cook for 5 minutes over medium-low flame on camp stove. Drizzle over pancakes or serve on the side.

Mango-Kiwi Relish

Ingredients
2 ripe mangos
4 ripe kiwi fruit

Directions
Cut mango in half on either side of the seed. Score fruit with a sharp knife in a small cube pattern in both directions without cutting through skin. Turn mango half inside out, then cut fruit away from skin into a bowl. Peel kiwis and cut into cubes the same size as mango. Top each pancake with about 1 to 2 tablespoons of cubed fruit.

Tip: You can cook these pancakes over your morning fire by waiting until you have a good coal bed, then placing your Tuscan grill over the fire topped with a cast iron griddle. Use the smooth side of the griddle brushed with oil or butter. You can make many more pancakes at one time using this method.

The Gourmet Girls
Go Camping

Amazing meals straight from your campfire!

By Gail Kearns, Denise Woodrey, and Shelley Mitchell

Gourmet Girls
on Fire

Leisurely Lunch

I f you must bring cold cuts along, make them the good ones. Order your sliced deli meats from an actual deli counter. You can immediately taste the difference between fresh cuts and the prepackaged monotony residing in the grocery store's cold case. The latter have been found to contain a higher concentration of fat and sodium. Also, any opportunity to leave preservatives in the dust, we'll take it! We feel similarly about bread. Buy it fresh. You are already putting your food to the test by leaving it in a cooler for days on end, so starting out fresh will mean a more palatable experience all around.

Camping for most people is also a vacation, so we understand wanting some lazy days sitting around the campsite and snuggling up with your favorite book. There are also instances where you'll want to bring your lunch along for a jaunt through the wilderness. While packing for your trip, make sure to include a bunch of trail-worthy snacks: apples, carrot sticks, and a little plate of cheese and pâté should do the trick. If you're planning on stuffing your gourmet lunch into a backpack or beach bag, use hard plastic containers for sandwiches and other squishables so they don't come out looking like a facelift gone wrong.

❧ Black Bean and Goat Cheese Quesadillas ❧
(CS)

Mango-peach salsa can be made ahead of time at home. Or, you might find a store-bought salsa to substitute. You probably won't find anything like our homemade version, but let us know if you do!

Makes 36 wedges

Ingredients
2 tablespoons olive oil
1 medium onion, chopped
1 teaspoon ground cumin
2 16-ounce cans refried black beans
12 large flour tortillas
6 to 8 ounces goat cheese
Cilantro leaves, to taste
Unsalted butter
Mango-Peach Salsa (page 195)

Directions
Sauté chopped onion and cumin in olive oil until onion is golden brown. Mix together the cooked onions and refried black beans. Spread 6 of the tortillas with the bean mixture. Sprinkle each bean surface with about 2 tablespoons crumbled goat cheese and cilantro leaves. Cover with remaining tortillas. Melt 2½ teaspoons butter over low heat in a 10-inch sauté pan, tipping the pan to evenly coat the bottom with butter. Sauté each quesadilla over medium heat about 1 to 2 minutes per side, adding butter as needed until tortillas are golden brown and cheese has melted. Wrap quesadillas in foil and keep warm.

When all the quesadillas have been sautéed, place them on a flat board. Cut each quesadilla in half, and then cut each half into 3 wedges. Top each wedge with a generous teaspoon of salsa and place on a serving platter. Serve immediately.

⋙ Chicken Salad with Apple, Dill, and Capers ⋘

This is the perfect make-ahead luncheon dish that will delight your fellow campers on your first day after arrival.

Serves 6

Ingredients
1 roasted chicken
1 bunch fresh dill, chopped
1 4-ounce jar small capers
2 green onions, chopped fine
2 Granny Smith apples, cut into medium dice
Juice and zest of one lemon
Salt and pepper
½ cup mayonnaise

Directions
Cut apart roasted chicken and take off all the skin. Cut meat into small to medium cubes or shred. Place in bowl and set aside. Add the dill, capers, green onions, apple, lemon juice and zest, salt and pepper to the chicken. Then add mayonnaise to taste, and mix well. Store in an airtight container or large resealable bag and refrigerate until ready to transfer to cooler. This salad will last about three days in your cooler. Serve on a bed of fresh arugula or lettuce, or enjoy all by itself.

Tip: If you don't like dark meat in your chicken salad, leave it out for another use and only use the breast meat.

⋑ Curried Egg Salad Sandwiches ⋐

This is an easy timesaving make-ahead recipe!

Serves 4

Ingredients

8 hardboiled eggs
4 tablespoons mayonnaise
1 clove garlic, pressed (optional)
2 tablespoons curry powder
Salt and pepper to taste

Sliced Havarti cheese
2 heirloom tomatoes, sliced
Fresh arugula
8 pieces of your favorite bread

Directions

Make ahead: Boil 8 eggs for 10 minutes. Place pan in sink and run cold water into pan with cooked eggs until eggs are cool. Remove from water and place in refrigerator to chill. When well chilled, remove eggs from refrigerator and shell them. Place shelled eggs into a medium-sized bowl and, using two knives, cut them up until the pieces are about ½ inch in size or smaller. Add the mayonnaise, the pressed garlic, curry powder, and salt and pepper. Mix together thoroughly until curry powder is fully incorporated. Place egg salad in a container and place in refrigerator until ready to transfer to your cooler.

At the campsite: Assemble your sandwiches by spreading 2 tablespoons of egg salad onto 1 slice of bread. Add a slice of Havarti cheese, a slice of heirloom tomato, and a handful of arugula. Top with another slice of bread and chow down.

≋ Genoa-Style Minestrone with Pesto ≋ (CS)

A great recipe for a fall camping trip! Make the pesto ahead of time at home.

Serves 8

Ingredients
½ cup olive oil, plus ¼ cup
1 leek, white part, cleaned and coarsely chopped
1 medium-sized red onion, chopped
3 medium-sized celery stalks, chopped
1 large boiling potato, peeled and cut into ½-inch pieces
3 medium-sized carrots, peeled and cut lengthwise into quarters
1 ripe tomato, peeled and seeded
Handful of fresh Italian parsley, chopped
1 cup beef broth
Salt and pepper, to taste
½ pound short tubular dried pasta
1 can cannellini beans

Make ahead: Pesto
Ingredients
¼ cup walnuts
1 tablespoon pine nuts
½ cup olive oil
1½ cups loosely packed fresh basil leaves
2 medium-sized cloves garlic, peeled
4 ounces freshly grated Parmesan cheese
Salt and pepper, to taste

Directions
Put the walnuts, pine nuts, basil, garlic, and ¼ cup oil in a blender or food processor and grind until very fine. Add the remaining ¼ cup oil and blend all the ingredients together until smooth. Transfer to a storage container. Add Parmesan, salt and pepper and mix together. Cover and refrigerate until ready to pack up.

At the campsite: Heat ¼ cup olive oil in a stockpot and add the chopped ingredients, potato, and carrots. Sauté for 5 minutes. Add the tomato and sauté for 5 minutes longer. Add broth to the saucepot. Season with salt and pepper. Simmer, uncovered, for ½ hour. Raise heat under the stockpot until liquid comes to a boil. Add the pasta and cook until al dente, 9 to 12 minutes. Remove the stockpot from the heat. Drain the can of cannellini beans and add to the pot. Mix well. Add half of the pesto to the stockpot, stir very well, and serve immediately, adding some of the pesto to each serving.

⇒ Gourmet Grilled Cheese ⇐
(CS or TG)

Serves 4

Ingredients
8 slices dense sourdough bread, presliced
1 jar tomato jam (available at specialty food markets and on Amazon)
Smoked provolone cheese, sliced
New York cheddar cheese, sliced
Fontina cheese, sliced
2 avocados, sliced
2 heirloom tomatoes, sliced
Fresh arugula

Directions
Butter 1 side of 4 slices of sourdough bread. Place buttered side down on cast iron griddle set over a medium-hot fire or two burners of your camp stove. Spread with tomato jam and layer on cheese. Top with remaining 4 slices of bread. Lightly butter top piece of bread. When toasted on bottom and cheese has begun to melt, flip sandwiches carefully and toast other side. Remove from heat and plate sandwiches. Open them and add avocado, tomato, and arugula. Enjoy!

Variation: You can add prosciutto or Black Forest ham to the sandwich before you top with second piece of bread if you would like a nonvegetarian version.

⋛ James Ranch Veggie Burger ⋚
(CS)

This recipe is adapted from the James Ranch and Harvest Grill in Durango, Colorado.

Serves 4

Ingredients
Olive oil
1 large yellow onion
2 to 3 small round summer squash (sometimes called sunburst or orbit squash)
Salt and pepper
Thyme
1 large tomato
4 brioche buns
Good melting cheese (Belford, available from James Ranch) or a soft Gouda, grated
Homemade Rosemary Garlic Mayonnaise (page 193)

Directions
Caramelize onions by slowly cooking them in a little olive oil until they are richly browned (about 30 to 45 minutes). Stir frequently. If they start to burn, add a teaspoon of water.

Cut squash into ¼-inch rounds. Sprinkle with salt and pepper to taste. Add a few sprigs of thyme to each round. Sauté in frying pan on cook stove.

Slice the tomato and grate the cheese.

Cut brioche buns in half and spread with rosemary garlic mayonnaise. Assemble sandwich, placing the caramelized onions on top.

Tip: Caramelize a big batch of yellow onions and reheat for your evening burgers.

⇌ Maury's BLT Deluxe ⇋
(CS or TG)

If you've got the time, precook the bacon at home. When ready to put together the BLTs at the campsite, you can reheat the bacon on your cook stove.

Serves 4

Ingredients
12 slices Trader Joe's uncured Black Forest Bacon
Unsalted butter
8 slices dense sourdough bread, presliced
Organic mayonnaise
2 avocados, sliced
Point Reyes Farmstead cheese, sliced
2 heirloom tomatoes, sliced
3 handfuls arugula
Trader Joe's aioli garlic mustard

Make ahead: Precook bacon, cool, and store in an airtight container.

At the campsite: Butter 1 side of 4 slices of sourdough bread. Place buttered side down on cast iron griddle set over a medium-hot fire or two burners of your camp stove. Spread with organic mayonnaise and layer on bacon, avocados, cheese, tomatoes, and arugula. Top with remaining 4 slices of bread that have been spread with aioli garlic mustard. Lightly butter topside of bread. When toasted on bottom and cheese has begun to melt, flip sandwiches carefully and toast other side.

❧ Neecie's Pork Tacos ❧
(TG)

Serves 4 (2 tacos each)

Ingredients
2 tablespoons olive oil
1 medium onion, julienned
2 cups mushrooms, cleaned and cut in half
Heavy duty aluminum foil
1 pork loin
2 cloves garlic, pressed
Salt and pepper to taste
8 white corn tortillas or premade taco shells
2 cups grated pepper jack cheese
2 cups lettuce or baby arugula, shredded
2 cups fresh cilantro leaves
2 cups prepared pico de gallo or other salsa

Directions
In 2 tablespoons olive oil, sauté onion for 10 minutes until slightly browned. Add mushrooms and sauté another 5 minutes. Set aside.

Cut two lengths of heavy duty aluminum foil 4 inches longer on each end than the pork loin. Place loin on one piece of foil. Rub pressed garlic over loin, then top with salt, pepper, sautéed onions, and mushrooms. Drizzle with olive oil. Place second piece of foil over seasoned loin and vegetables and seal lengthwise along top and bottom. Fold in each end of foil, sealing well.

Place Tuscan grill over a medium-hot bed of coals in the firepit. Place foil packet of pork on Tuscan grill. Be careful not to tear foil. Cook for 20 minutes.

Remove foil packet from grill and place on a platter. Carefully open packet. Hot steam will escape so proceed with caution! When cool enough to handle, turn meat out onto a cutting board and chop into bite-sized pieces. Mix in onions and mushrooms. Keep warm.

Warm 8 corn tortillas over Tuscan grill. When warm, assemble tacos placing meat/veggie combo in center of a tortilla, top with cheese, then with remaining ingredients. Alternately, you can use a taco rack to build and warm tacos on the grill. It's an excellent way to melt the cheese and then add the cold toppings before eating.

Variation: If you have the time and really want to make a crunchy, light-as-air taco shell, you can fry the white corn tortillas in hot peanut oil, 3 inches deep. This takes practice, as you have to hold one half of the tortilla out of the oil and bend it into a taco shape, being careful to keep a 2-inch gap between the edges of the tortilla and not to spill the oil. Use tongs for this. You can only do one at a time, but they cook really fast, so be careful not to burn them. When the first side is golden brown, turn the uncooked side down into the oil, again being careful to keep the mouth of the taco shell open. When both sides are golden brown, remove and drain on paper towels. The secret here is that your oil has to be really hot. After draining, the shells should not be at all greasy.

⮃ Yvonne's Asian Noodle Salad ⮃
(CS)

Adapted from "The Pioneer Woman" *recipe.*

Serves 4–6

Ingredients
1 package soba noodles, cooked, rinsed, and cooled
½ head napa cabbage, sliced
½ head purple cabbage, sliced
4 to 5 spears baby bok choy, slivered
1 red bell pepper, sliced thinly
1 yellow bell pepper, sliced thinly
1 orange bell pepper, sliced thinly
1 bag bean sprouts (also called mung bean sprouts)
1 bunch cilantro, chopped
3 whole scallions, sliced
3 whole cucumbers, sliced
⅓ bag of Trader Joe's Thai Lime & Chili Cashews, crushed

Dressing
1 lime, juiced
8 tablespoons olive oil
8 tablespoons soy sauce
2 to 3 tablespoons sesame oil
⅓ cup brown sugar
3 tablespoons fresh ginger, minced
2 cloves garlic, minced
1 to 2 hot peppers (jalapeño or serrano), seeded and finely diced
Cilantro, chopped

Directions

Mix together salad ingredients in a large bowl. Whisk dressing ingredients and pour over salad. Toss with tongs and serve on a platter.

Tip: Keep the dressing for up to three days in the refrigerator, without cilantro. Add cilantro immediately before serving.

Variation: You may replace the soba noodles with linguine or angel hair pasta. Add cooked shrimp, chicken, or Marinated Tofu for Grilling (page 147) to this noodle salad for a tasty dinner entrée on a warm evening.

The Main Event

By now you're a few fabulous cocktails in, and the appetizers are sitting happily in your fire-warmed belly. This is the exact moment when you'll thank yourself for all the at-home prep work. Time to pull things out of your perfectly packed cooler and finish the job.

You're likely to end up with leftovers from some of these awesome recipes, so make sure to bring a few extra containers for later enjoyment. We've been known to use leftover pork from Seyburn's Barbecued Tandoori Pork Loin with Jajik recipe (page 139) the next day for lunch in Neecie's Pork Tacos (page 88). The last day of our camping trips involve everyone opening up their coolers and devouring the leftovers from the entire trip as we pack up our gear.

If you haven't already made your camp neighbors jealous, the imminent smell of garlic and onions sautéing in butter will definitely do the trick. Their prepackaged hamburger patties and dried-out hot dog buns have got nothing on these campfire compadres. Any good cook knows how to follow a recipe, but real cooks tend to experiment. After a day or two of awesome meals, your neighbors will likely come sniffing around with their mouths drooling. See if you can convince them to let you use their fire ring for dinner prep in exchange for a little savory treat. It will double your cooking surface and your chances of finding a new gin rummy opponent.

➽ Asian Style Halibut en Papillote ➽
(DO)

Serves 2

Ingredients
4 12-inch square pieces of parchment paper
2 tablespoons coconut oil, one for spreading on parchment and one for sautéing leeks
6 hefty asparagus spears
1 large leek, sliced thinly
6 shiitake mushrooms, sliced thinly
2 fillets of Alaskan wild-caught halibut, 1½ inch thick
2 tablespoons ponzu (citrus-based soy sauce)
2 tablespoons mirin (Asian sweet rice wine)
Splash of sesame oil
Salt and pepper to taste

Directions
Prepare a coal fire for Dutch oven cooking at 325°F (see chart, page 23).

Peel the bottom of the asparagus and cut spears in half lengthwise.

Sauté leeks in 1 tablespoon coconut oil until golden. Set aside.

Place half of the asparagus, shiitake mushrooms, and leeks on one piece of parchment paper coated with coconut oil. Place halibut on top. Sprinkle with ponzu sauce, mirin, and a splash of sesame oil. Add salt and pepper to taste. Place a second piece of parchment over halibut and fold all sides in to seal the packet. Repeat with remaining ingredients to make second packet.

Place trivet in the bottom of a Dutch oven. Carefully place fish packets on top of trivet and bake halibut 10 to 15 minutes with lid on.

Tip: To test for doneness, insert a bamboo skewer through the parchment and into the thickest part of the fish. If you feel any resistance, it needs another couple of minutes to cook. Do not overcook! It's better to pull the fish off of the heat early and let it continue to cook in the packet.

Alternate condiments
Papaya, cut into small pieces
Blackberries, whole
Lemon, thinly sliced
Lime, thinly sliced
Chives, snipped
Cilantro, chopped fine
Fennel pollen
Balsamic glaze
Salt and pepper

⮂ Campfire Salmon with Lemon Dill Cream Sauce ⮀ (TG)

Meet Wilbur, the 13.5-pound salmon and our original test subject pictured to the right. This surprisingly easy recipe produces an incredibly flavorful tender meal that can serve your entire campsite. We recommend inviting your camp host over for this one.

Serves 10–12

Ingredients

10 pounds whole fresh salmon, packed in ice

4 sheets aluminum foil (6 inches longer than length of salmon)

Coconut oil or nonstick cooking spray

1 large onion, sliced, or 2 leeks separated into leaves

2 lemons

2 tablespoons Herbs de Provence or similar dry seasoning

2 cups fresh herbs, coarsely chopped (basil, cilantro, oregano, dill, etc.)

Lemon Dill Cream Sauce (page 194)

Directions

Rinse any ice glaze from salmon under cold water and pat dry. Lay out 2 sheets of aluminum foil, double thickness. Coat top layer with coconut oil or nonstick cooking spray. Lay half of the onions lengthwise across foil. Place salmon over onions. Squeeze lemon on both sides of fish. Sprinkle dry seasoning onto salmon. Place fresh herbs over, under, and into the belly cavity. Lay out remaining two sheets of foil, double thickness, and coat top layer with coconut oil or nonstick cooking spray and place coated side face down onto herbs and salmon. Roll up, crimp, and seal all sides to form packet. Cook salmon over medium grill (400°F) 5 to 6 inches from heat for 1 hour, turning packet over every 15 minutes. Cook until only a tiny bit of translucency is left in the center; the fish will finish cooking off the grill. Remove pieces and drizzle with lemon dill cream sauce.

Tip: Scale the fish before cooking, using a thin-bladed knife held at an angle. Scrape from tail to head to remove scales. Rinse fish. We recommend getting your fishmonger to do this for you!

⋙ Grilled Trout Wrapped in Bacon ⋘
(TG)

Serves 2–4

Ingredients
2 rainbow trout (12 to 14 ounces each) butterflied, bones removed
Smoked sea salt
Pepper to taste
½ cup chopped fresh herbs (dill, parsley, thyme, sage, etc.)
6 slices thin bacon
Lemons as garnish

Directions
Prepare grill for medium heat.

Season trout inside and out with salt and pepper, going easy on the smoked sea salt. It imparts a wonderful flavor, but it can be strong.

Stuff the cavities of the trout with herbs.

Wrap each trout with 3 slices of bacon.

Grill trout 10 to 15 minutes in a reliable fish basket, turning frequently (1 to 2 minutes) to avoid flare-ups as much as possible. Bacon should be crisp.

Serve with lemon wedges.

Tip: Most fishmongers and specialty fish markets will have trout already butterflied and deboned. Check with yours when you're fishing around for trout!

⤳ Grilled Whole Branzino ⤳
(TG)

Serves 2

Ingredients

2 whole branzino, each 1 to 1½ pounds, scaled, cleaned, and fins removed
½ lemon, sliced thinly
1 garlic clove, sliced thinly

3 sprigs rosemary, thyme, or other herbs
Salt and pepper
Olive oil
Lemon wedges for serving

Directions

Prepare grill for medium–high heat. Season inside of fish with salt and pepper. Stuff each cavity with mixed herbs, lemon slices, and garlic. Drizzle the outside of the fish with olive oil. Fit branzino securely into a fish grill basket.

Place the fish basket on the grill. Cook, turning once or twice until skin is crisp and flesh is flaky and opaque down to the bone, about 5 minutes per side. (If a small knife slides easily through the thickest part of flesh, the fish is done.)

Tip: If you're relaxing around the campsite, this makes a delicious lunch with our Grilled Peach and Prosciutto Salad recipe (page 162).

⇛ Linguine with Clams and Mussels Oreganata ⇚
(CS)

Serves 4–6

Ingredients

2 pounds frozen clams or an equal amount of fresh clams

2 pounds frozen mussels or equal amount of fresh mussels

1 pound dried linguine

2 tablespoons butter

1 to 2 tablespoons olive oil

4 cloves garlic, sliced thinly

¼ cup (or so) white wine

2 lemons

Pinch of red pepper flakes

2 tablespoons fresh oregano, chopped

¼ cup fresh flat-leaf parsley, finely chopped

Bottled clam juice, if needed

½ cup finely grated Parmesan

Salt and pepper to taste

Directions

Scrub clams and mussels in a tub of water, if using fresh. Change water once or twice. Cook the linguine according to the package. Heat butter and oil in a pan and add the garlic. Cook the garlic until soft and fragrant. Deglaze the pan with the wine. Cook until liquid is reduced. Add clams and mussels and allow them to open, about 5 minutes. Discard any that do not open. When cool enough to handle, remove at least half of clam and mussel meat from their shells. You can chop or leave whole. Juices from the clams and mussels should provide enough liquid for the sauce. If not, add desired amount of bottled clam juice.

Remove pan from heat and add cooked linguine, juice of half a lemon, pepper flakes, fresh oregano, and parsley. Add salt and pepper, to taste. Serve with lemon wedges and Parmesan cheese.

Tip: Try to find the PanaPesca frozen clams and mussels, available in many supermarkets and specialty stores across the United States. They are precooked, all natural, and clean as a whistle. Keep them on ice in your cooler and use them the first night of your camping trip.

⊜ Lobster Boil ⊜
(CS)

Serves 3–4

Ingredients

1 large onion, quartered

8 small, whole Yukon Gold potatoes

1 head of garlic

3 links of smoked kielbasa sausages, cut into 2½-inch pieces

3 whole live lobsters

2 pounds of clams

5 ears of corn, shucked and halved

Directions

Fill a large stockpot with water. The pot should be large enough to fit the lobsters with plenty of room. Add a tablespoon of salt to the water and bring to a boil. Quarter the onion and cut the head of garlic through the widest part of the head. Add to the boiling water. Add potatoes and cook for about 8 minutes. Then add kielbasa. Snip rubber bands off the lobster claws. Add lobsters to the boiling water.

Cook lobsters, uncovered, according to weight (see below for timing based on weight). Divide the clams in half and tie up each half loosely with cheesecloth. Make sure there is room for the clams to open. Seven minutes before the lobsters are done cooking, add the clams. Three minutes before lobsters are done cooking, add the corn.

Remove lobsters and allow to cool for 10 minutes. Strain the boil and arrange on a platter. Serve with lemon wedges and melted butter.

Cooking Time for Lobster

1 pound = 8 minutes

1¼ pounds = 9-10 minutes

1½ pounds = 11-12 minutes

1¾ pounds = 12-13 minutes

2 pounds = 15 minutes

2½ pounds = 20 minutes

⋙ Paella on the Grill ⋘
(V)

Serves 8

Ingredients
¼ cup extra virgin olive oil
2 pounds chicken thighs
1 pound dry cured chorizo, cut into half-moons
1 medium onion, peeled and finely chopped
1 tablespoon minced garlic
4 cups paella rice, such as Matiz or Bomba
½ cup white wine
2¼ quarts chicken broth
One large pinch saffron
8 to 10 sea scallops
2 dozen littleneck clams, cleaned
Slices of pimento for garnish
Salt and freshly ground black pepper
2 tablespoons finely chopped parsley
Lemon wedges for serving

Directions
Prepare Volcano grill for medium-high heat. In an 18-inch paella pan, heat the olive oil. Season the chicken thighs with salt and pepper and brown on all sides in the hot oil. Transfer to a plate. Cook the chorizo in the same pan until it starts to brown. Transfer to a second, paper-towel-lined plate.

Add onion to the pan and cook until translucent, about 4 minutes. Add the garlic and stir until fragrant, then add the rice and stir to coat. Season with salt and pepper. Add ½ cup of white wine, stir, and let wine evaporate. Heat a bit of chicken stock and infuse with saffron.

Fire should now be at its peak heat. Quickly stir the chorizo into the rice, then slowly add 2 quarts of stock along with saffron-infused stock. Move the rice mixture around gently until it is evenly distributed throughout the pan. It's important not to stir the rice after this point. After about 10 minutes add the scallops and clams hinge-side up so that when they open in the heat, their juices are released into the rice. Nestle the chicken on top.

Cook the paella until all the liquid has absorbed, 25 to 30 minutes. If the rice is underdone, add another cup of stock and return to the fire for 5 to 7 minutes. Lay strips of pimento on the paella. Season with salt and pepper to taste and top with parsley. Remove from heat and cover with aluminum foil. Let sit 10 minutes, then serve with lemon wedges.

Tip: Easier than you think! You just need to make sure you have your mise en place together before you stoke up the Volcano.

⮕ Pan-Seared Swordfish Steaks ⮔
(CS)

Serves 2

Ingredients
2 1-inch-thick swordfish steaks, each about 6 ounces
1 tablespoon unsalted butter
½ tablespoon olive oil
3 shallots, sliced thinly
¼ cup dry white wine
2 tablespoons balsamic vinegar
1 tablespoon drained capers, chopped
1 tablespoon water
1 tablespoon fresh parsley, chopped

Directions
Pat swordfish dry and season with salt and pepper. In a heavy skillet, heat butter and oil over moderately high heat until foam subsides and sauté shallots with salt to taste, stirring, 1 minute. Push shallots to side of skillet.

Add swordfish and sauté until golden, about 3 minutes. Turn fish over and add wine, vinegar, capers, and water. Simmer mixture 3 minutes or until fish is just cooked through.

Transfer fish to 2 plates and stir parsley into sauce. Spoon sauce over fish.

Tip: The key to pan searing is making sure the pan is hot enough. To test a pan for readiness, sprinkle a drop of water onto the pan. If the water sizzles, you are good to go!

⋙ Petrale Sole Almondine ⋘
(CS)

Serves 4

Ingredients

1 cup blanched slivered almonds
3 tablespoons butter
1 tablespoon extra virgin olive oil
4 petrale sole fillets
Flour, for dredging
2 eggs

1 cup Trader Joe's Organic Bread Crumbs or panko
2 shallots, finely chopped
1 cup white wine
1 lemon, juiced
¼ cup flat-leaf parsley, chopped
Salt and pepper

Directions

Toast almonds in a skillet until golden brown, about 5 to 7 minutes. Season with salt and set aside. Return pan to medium heat. Add 2 tablespoons butter and 1 tablespoon olive oil. Dredge fillets in flour seasoned with salt and pepper, then dip into eggs. Allow some of the excess egg to drain off. Coat both sides of fillets with breadcrumbs or panko, pressing down gently. Fry 2 fillets at a time for 1 to 2 minutes per side and take fillets out of pan. Loosely cover with foil and set aside.

Sauté shallots until translucent. Deglaze pan with white wine and lemon. Cook down for 3 to 5 minutes. Add 1 tablespoon butter. Plate the fillets and pour over sauce. Sprinkle with parsley and almonds.

Variation: If you can find them, sand dabs are an excellent alternative to sole. They are a delicacy and one of California's better-kept seafood secrets. There are probably many ways they could be cooked, but the only way we've ever done a dab is to pan fry it. It's almost like they were designed to this end. Bread crumbs, a little egg wash, and drop 'em in the hot skillet. Yummy!

⪦ Planked Salmon with Blood Orange Sauce ⪧
(TG)

Serves 4

Ingredients
1 to 2 cedar planks, soaked at least 1 hour
4 salmon fillets with skin
3 to 4 blood oranges
1 large shallot
1 tablespoon butter
¼ cup of sake
2 tablespoons soy sauce
¼ cup honey
1 tablespoon Trader Joe's Orange Muscat Champagne Vinegar
Salt and pepper to taste

Directions
Prepare grill for high heat. Slice two of the blood oranges into ¼-inch wheels. Place the salmon on the soaked planks and salt and pepper the salmon to taste. Place them onto the grill and grill for about 15 minutes along with cut orange slices from 2 or 3 of the oranges. Remove orange slices when grill marks are made on both sides.

Finely chop the shallot and sauté in butter in a saucepan. Squeeze the juice from the remaining orange, or two if they are small, into the pan. Add the sake, soy, honey, and muscat vinegar. Bring to a simmer until it thickens up and reduces a little. This takes about 7 to 10 minutes. Brush sauce onto salmon while grilling. Top the salmon with grilled orange slices before serving.

Variation: If blood oranges are not available, you can use any juice orange. Squeeze a bit of lemon into the sauce. You can also add a bit of zest from the oranges and lemon.

➤ Shrimp and Sausage Skewers with Smoky Paprika Glaze ➤ (TG or V)

This recipe was adapted from Epicurious.

Serves 4–6

Ingredients

¾ cup olive oil
4 large garlic cloves, pressed
2 tablespoons chopped fresh thyme
5 teaspoons smoked paprika
4 teaspoons sherry wine vinegar
¾ teaspoon salt or smoked salt to taste
½ teaspoon freshly ground black pepper
½ teaspoon dried crushed red pepper

12 uncooked extra-large shrimp (13 to 15 per pound), peeled and deveined
12 1-inch-long pieces andouille or other fully cooked smoked sausage (such as Italian sweet sausage or chorizo, if you want spicy)
12 cherry tomatoes
12 2-layer sections of red onion wedges
Nonstick vegetable oil spray

Directions

To make the glaze: Whisk oil, garlic, thyme, smoked paprika, sherry wine vinegar, salt, black pepper, and crushed red pepper in medium bowl. Transfer half of glaze to small bowl and reserve for serving.

Alternately thread shrimp, sausage pieces, cherry tomatoes, and sections of onion wedges on each of 6 long metal or bamboo skewers. Arrange skewers on a large rimmed baking sheet. Coat grill rack with nonstick spray and prepare barbecue for medium-high heat. Brush skewers on both sides with glaze from 1 bowl. Grill until shrimp are opaque in center, turning and brushing occasionally with more glaze, 6 to 8 minutes. Arrange skewers on platter. Serve with remaining bowl of glaze.

Tip: If you're using bamboo skewers instead of metal, be sure to soak them for at least 1 hour before threading them with ingredients and grilling.

⪼ Skewered Scallops Wrapped in Bacon with Maple Syrup Glaze ⪻
(TG or V)

Serves 4

Ingredients
12 slices applewood smoked bacon or other thick-cut bacon
12 sea scallops
5 tablespoons maple syrup
1 tablespoon Dijon mustard
12 bamboo skewers, soaked in water for 1 hour or more
Salt
Freshly ground black pepper

Directions
Partially cook bacon in a skillet for 3 to 5 minutes. Drain on paper towels.

Season scallops with salt and pepper. Wrap each scallop with 1 piece of bacon, securing it through the center with a bamboo skewer. Repeat with remaining scallops.

Mix maple syrup and Dijon mustard together. Coat the bacon-wrapped scallops with the maple syrup mixture.

Prepare a grill for medium-high heat. When the grill is hot, brush the grates lightly with oil, then place the scallops on the grill and cook, turning frequently, until just cooked through, about 7 minutes.

Tip: Skewered scallops also make a great appetizer!

⋙ Bourbon-Molasses Glazed Cornish Game Hens ⋘
(V)

Marinate hens ahead of time at home. This is not only a timesaver but also it improves their flavor and tenderizes the meat.

Serves 4

Ingredients

2 Cornish game hens, split lengthwise (directions below)
2 cloves garlic, minced
1 tablespoon olive oil
1 cup catsup
½ cup chicken broth

½ cup bourbon
¼ cup molasses
¼ cup firmly packed brown sugar
1 teaspoon mustard
1 teaspoon fresh ginger, minced
¼ teaspoon cayenne

Directions

Make ahead: Place the hens on a cutting board and split down the middle of the breast and through the backbone with a large, heavy chef's knife. Place hen half bone side down on cutting board and press down hard on it to flatten it out. Do this to both hens, then place the four halves in a large resealable bag. (You may need to place two in one bag and two in another.)

In a 4 to 5 quart pan, combine garlic and oil. Stir often over medium-high heat until lightly browned, about 10 minutes.

Add catsup, broth, bourbon, molasses, brown sugar, mustard, ginger, and cayenne. Mix well. Bring to a boil, then simmer, stirring often, until reduced to 1⅓ cups, about 20 minutes. It should look dark and thickened. Let cool, and then chill for up to 3 days or until ready to transfer to cooler.

At the campsite: Remove hens from cooler and bring to forest temperature.

Prepare a charcoal fire in your Volcano grill. Pat the hen halves dry, and when coals are spotted with gray ash, place the hen halves bone side down on grill. Cook on this side for 20 minutes, covered, then turn them over and cook for another 15 minutes covered.

Uncover Volcano and brush birds generously with sauce. Continue cooking, turning, and basting with more sauce until meat near thighbone is no longer pink (cut to test), about 20 minutes. When done, remove from heat and let rest for 5 minutes. Serve and enjoy!

⇒ Camping Coq Au Vin ⇐
(DO)

Serves 4

Ingredients

6 slices bacon, diced into ½-inch pieces

4 chicken leg quarters or 2 whole small chickens cut into 4 pieces

1 lb button mushrooms (white or cremini)

¼ cup all-purpose flour

2 tablespoons tomato paste

8 ounces pearl onions (see tip below)

½ cup shallots, minced

4 medium clove garlics, crushed

3 medium carrots, diced

3 cups of dry red wine (we like a fairly good Pinot Noir)

6 sprigs fresh thyme

1 bay leaf

2 cups chicken broth

Directions

Prepare a coal fire for Dutch oven cooking at 350°F (see chart, page 23). Place Dutch oven over 12 hot coals and fry bacon until crisp. Transfer bacon to paper towels and let drain. Season chicken with salt and pepper. Add chicken skin side down and cook until browned. Add mushrooms to Dutch oven, stirring frequently, until browned, about 10 minutes. Add flour and tomato paste and cook, stirring constantly, for 1 minute. Add pearl onions, shallots, garlic, and carrots and cook until lightly browned. Add bacon, wine, thyme, and bay leaf and bring to a simmer. Stir in stock. Bring liquid back to a simmer. Place lid on pan, add required number of coals to top of lid, and cook for 1 hour.

Tip: Frozen pearl onions can be tossed into your cooler and used in place of fresh. Keep them in the coldest part of the cooler, and if they've defrosted a bit by the time you use them, that's okay. Just drain and add them to the Dutch oven about halfway through the cooking process.

⇌ Dutch Oven Chicken Marbella ⇋
(DO)

The Silver Palate Cookbook *inspired this recipe. Marinating the chicken at home before heading out to the campsite is a good timesaver.*

Serves 10–12 (Cut ingredients in half to make smaller amount)

Ingredients
4 chickens quartered or 6 thighs, drumsticks, and breast halves, bone in
6 cloves of garlic, peeled and pressed
¼ cup dried oregano
Salt and freshly ground black pepper, to taste
½ cup red wine vinegar
½ cup olive oil
1 cup pitted prunes
6 sliced shallots
½ cup pitted Spanish green olives
½ cup capers and a bit of juice
6 bay leaves
1 cup brown sugar
1 cup white wine
¼ cup finely chopped Italian flat-leaf parsley or cilantro

Directions

Make ahead: In a large bowl combine chicken, garlic, oregano, pepper, salt to taste, vinegar, olive oil, prunes, olives, capers and juice, and bay leaves. Place in large resealable bag and let marinate overnight in the fridge. The next morning, when you are ready to leave for your camping trip, transfer to cooler.

At the campsite: Prepare coals for Dutch oven cooking at 350°F (see chart, page 23). Arrange chicken in layers and pour over marinade evenly. Sprinkle chicken with brown sugar and pour in white wine.

Cook 45 minutes to 1 hour, checking frequently and rotating pieces of chicken to prevent scorching. Chicken is done when thigh pieces, pricked with a fork at their thickest area, yield clear yellow (rather than pink) juices.

With a slotted spoon, transfer chicken, prunes, olives, and capers to a serving platter. Moisten with a few spoonfuls of pan juices and sprinkle generously with parsley or cilantro. Pass remaining pan juices in a sauceboat.

Tip: To serve Chicken Marbella cold, cool to forest temperature in cooking juices before transferring to a serving platter. Spoon some of the reserved juice over chicken and you have what we call pure picnic bliss!

⇒ Chicken Skewers Moroccan Style ⇐
(TG or V)

Make the marinade ahead at home and infuse the chicken with it overnight.

Serves 4

Ingredients

4 garlic cloves, pressed
2 tablespoons good yogurt
¼ to ½ teaspoon harissa powder
2 teaspoons ground cumin
1 tablespoon white wine
⅓ cup olive oil
Fresh or dried cilantro
Salt to taste

8 bamboo skewers
1 pound chicken thighs and breast meat
1 onion, sliced quarterly
8 tricolored baby bell peppers (or 1 large red bell pepper)
10 to 12 small white or cremini mushrooms, left whole

Directions

Make ahead: In a large bowl, whisk together garlic, yogurt, harissa powder, cumin, and white wine. Slowly add olive oil, continuing to whisk. Add cilantro and salt to taste. Add chicken thighs and breast meat and toss. Place in leakproof resealable bag and refrigerate overnight until ready to transfer to cooler.

At the campsite: Soak bamboo skewers in water for 1 hour. Cut chicken into 2-inch cubes. Cut baby bell peppers in half, or red bell pepper into 2-inch pieces. When ready, thread onions, peppers, mushrooms, and chicken pieces onto skewers.

Oil grill grates. Place skewers on grill over medium-high heat, basting and turning occasionally until done, about 20 to 25 minutes.

⇒ Indian Spiced Chicken ⇐
(DO)

Recipe courtesy of Marianna Åström-De Fina, an intrepid camper living in Sweden.

Serves 4

Ingredients

3 tablespoons unsalted butter
1 broiler/fryer chicken, cut into quarters
1 medium onion, chopped
1 medium leek, finely sliced
2 cloves fresh garlic, chopped fine
1 tablespoon fresh ginger, chopped
2 medium-sized Granny Smith green apples, chopped
1 tablespoon curry powder

1 tablespoon garam masala
½ tablespoon cayenne powder
4 cups chicken broth
½ cup tamari sauce
1 tablespoon red wine vinegar
½ cup Marcona almonds
2 bananas
½ cup coconut flakes, toasted

Directions

Place the coconut flakes in a small sauté pan and toast until light brown. Set aside. Prepare coals for Dutch oven to cook at 350°F. Arrange coals around the bottom of your Dutch oven and add half the butter. Brown the chicken pieces until skin is golden. Remove to a platter and set aside. Add remaining butter to Dutch oven and sauté the onions, finely sliced leeks, garlic, and ginger until onions are browned. Add the apple and spices and cook until the spices release their fragrance. Add the broth, tamari, and vinegar. Simmer 10 minutes.

Add the chicken pieces and almonds to the sauce and cover Dutch oven. Place six coals on top of Dutch oven and cook for 35 minutes or until chicken is done.

Serve topped with banana slices and toasted coconut flakes. Basmati rice and mango chutney are both wonderful accompaniments for this dish.

☙ Marinated Cornish Game Hens ❧
(V)

Marinating the hens at home saves you time. Shown left with Veggie Skewers (page 155) and Harvest Grains with Hazelnuts (page 183).

Serves 4

Ingredients

2 Cornish game hens, split lengthwise (directions below)

Juice and zest of 1 orange, 1 lime, and 1 Meyer lemon

2 cloves garlic, pressed

¼ cup cilantro, chopped

1 teaspoon honey

1 tablespoon soy sauce

½ cup peanut oil

1 tablespoon ginger, chopped

Directions

Make ahead: Place the hens on a cutting board and split down the middle of the breast and through the backbone with a large, heavy chef's knife. Place hen half bone side down on cutting board and press down hard on it to flatten it out. Do this to both hens, then place the four halves in a resealable bag. (You may need to place two in one bag and two in another.) Prepare the marinade by mixing together all of the rest of the ingredients. Pour it over the hens in the resealable bag. Refrigerate until ready to pack into your cooler.

At the campsite: Prepare a charcoal fire in your Volcano grill. When fire is too hot to keep your hand over it for 5 seconds, place the hen halves bone side down on grill. Cook on this side for 20 minutes, covered, then turn them over and cook for another 15 minutes uncovered. Test for doneness by cutting into the joint between the leg and thigh. If still pink, flip them over again and cover for another 10 minutes. When done, remove from heat and let rest for 5 minutes.

Tip: For a perfectly rounded meal, pair with our Harvest Grains with Hazelnuts (page 183), Mascarpone Polenta with Wild Mushrooms (page 184), and Grilled Caesar Salad (page 161).

⋑ Seared Duck Breast with Plums and Grenache Wine ⋐
(CS, TG)

Seasoning the duck ahead and leaving it in the fridge overnight helps to deepen the flavor and keeps work to a minimum at the campsite!

Serves 4

Ingredients

2 tablespoons soy sauce

1½ cups Grenache (divided)

1 shallot, minced

1 tablespoon fresh ginger, chopped

⅛ teaspoon red pepper flakes

¼ teaspoon cumin

1 teaspoon peanut oil

Salt and pepper

4 boneless duck breasts

1 tablespoon unsalted butter

2 plums (pits removed), quartered

1 cup chicken stock

Directions

Make ahead: Duck Marinade

In a small bowl combine the soy sauce, half a cup Grenache wine, shallots, ginger, red pepper flakes, cumin, peanut oil, and black pepper. Stir to combine.

Trim away the silver skin from the meat side of duck breast, and trim away any excess fat. Make diagonal cuts just through the skin at ¼-inch intervals. Place in resealable bag and marinate the duck skin side down for 1 hour before placing in refrigerator. Turn the breasts during the marinating.

Transfer to your cooler before leaving on your camping trip.

At the campsite: Heat butter in a small pan over medium heat on your camp stove. Add the plums. Season them with salt and pepper, tossing until they reach a nice brown. Remove the plums from the pan and put them to the side. Add the remaining cup of Grenache, the stock, and duck marinade. Bring to a boil, reduce heat to a simmer, and cook until the liquid is reduced by half and thickened. Add plums to sauce and continue to cook until plums are tender.

Prepare a wood fire in the firepit. Let fire die down and place Tuscan grill over the fire. Pat the breasts dry from the marinade and reserve. When fire is still too hot to keep your hand over it for 5 seconds, place them skin side down on grill. Cook on the skin side for 15 to 20 minutes or until skin is dark and the fat has rendered and skin is crisp. Turn over and cook for another 10 minutes or until meat is medium rare.

Spoon the plums and sauce onto the center of a plate and place the duck on top. This dish would be divine with our Mascarpone Polenta with Wild Mushrooms (page 184)!

⤳ Wonderbag Tender Roast Chicken ⤷
(W)

Imagine a way to slow cook your food when camping. You can prep everything after lunch and head to the trails. When you get back, presto! Getting dinner on has never been so easy. Or you can put it in the back of your car with no power, and have your meal already good to go when you arrive at your campsite.

Serves 4–6

Ingredients

1 whole chicken
1 tablespoon dried thyme
½ lemon
½ cup plain flour, seasoned with salt and pepper
3 tablespoons olive oil
10 garlic cloves, peeled and crushed
1 green chili, deseeded and finely chopped
1 onion, peeled and finely chopped
1 eggplant, chopped

1 carrot, peeled and finely chopped
½ green pepper, deseeded and finely chopped
2 tablespoons dried rosemary
1 can chopped tomatoes
2 tablespoons tomato puree
1 tablespoon vegetable stock powder
1 teaspoon apple cider vinegar
1 tablespoon brown sugar
½ cup chopped fresh parsley

Directions

Loosen the skin of the chicken and carefully spread the thyme in between the skin and meat. Place the lemon in the cavity.

Completely coat the chicken with the seasoned flour.

Heat the oil in a pot and fry the chicken until golden brown, turning continuously. Remove the chicken from the pot.

Add the garlic, chili, onion, eggplant, carrot, green pepper, and rosemary to the pot and fry gently for 5 minutes.

Add the tomatoes, tomato puree, stock powder, vinegar, and sugar, and bring to a boil. Cover and simmer for 15 minutes.

Place the chicken in the pot, breast down, and spoon some of the vegetable mixture over the chicken. Cover, bring to a boil, and boil gently for 30 minutes.

Place the lidded pot in the Wonderbag for 3 hours to finish cooking.

Garnish with chopped fresh parsley.

⪼ Beef and Pepper Skewers ⪻
(TG)

Both the Spiced Salt and Chimichurri Sauce can be made ahead at home.

Serves 4

Ingredients
1½ teaspoons cumin seeds
1½ teaspoons Sichuan peppercorns or ½
teaspoon black peppercorns
1 teaspoon kosher salt
½ teaspoon crushed red pepper flakes
1 pound flatiron steak, thinly sliced against
the grain

8 shishito peppers or Padrón chiles, halved
crosswise if large
2 tablespoons vegetable oil
Lime wedges (for serving)
Chimichurri Sauce (page 189)

Directions

Make ahead: Spiced Salt
Coarsely grind cumin seeds, Sichuan peppercorns, salt, and red pepper flakes in
a spice mill or mortar and pestle (you still want some pieces of spice). Store in an
airtight container at room temperature.

At the campsite: Soak bamboo skewers in water for 1 hour or longer. Prepare grill for
medium-high heat. Thread beef (fold over as needed to skewer) and peppers alternately onto
skewers, starting and ending with beef. Brush with oil and season with spiced salt. Grill,
turning often, until lightly charred and beef is medium-rare, 5 to 7 minutes. Serve with lime
wedges and chimichurri sauce.

Tip: The spiced salt is equally good on other cuts of meat, like chicken thighs or breasts and
pork chops. Make a big batch and use it as you like.

≳ Best (Blue Cheese) Burger Ever ≲
(TG or V)

Serves 4

Ingredients

2 pounds ground beef (80% lean), preferably ground sirloin steak tips or chuck
1 tablespoon garlic, minced
1 tablespoon fresh sage, crumbled
¾ teaspoon salt
1 teaspoon pepper

1 cup blue cheese, crumbled
Kaiser rolls or whole wheat hamburger buns
Condiments, such as sliced tomatoes, romaine, caramelized onions
Mayonnaise with a dash of Tabasco (optional) or any homemade spicy mayo

Directions

Place beef in a bowl along with minced garlic, sage, 1 teaspoon pepper, and ¾ teaspoon of salt over meat and gently toss with a fork to combine. Divide meat into eight balls. Gently flatten into patties.

In a separate bowl, form the crumbled cheese into four patties. Place one cheese patty on each of four beef patties. Top with remaining four beef patties, pinching the edges to seal the cheese completely. Transfer patties to your cooler for about 30 to 45 minutes.

Set up charcoal for grilling, using a chimney stack two-thirds filled with charcoal. When coals are partially covered with ash, spread them out in the firepit and set up the Tuscan grill. Get the grill hot and place the stuffed patties on the grill.

Cook patties without moving them until browned and meat easily releases from the grill. Flip patties and continue to cook to desired temperature.

Tip: Ask your butcher to grind the meat for you. It should be fine enough to ensure tenderness but coarse enough so the patties will stay loose. If buying chuck, have the butcher remove the connective tissue before grinding.

⋙ Bison Chili ⋘
(DO)

Serves 6–8

Ingredients
1 pound ground bison
1 large onion, finely chopped
1 large carrot, finely chopped
½ head cauliflower, stemmed and cut into small florets (about 3 cups)
1 medium red bell pepper, finely chopped
3 large garlic cloves, finely chopped
Bouquet garni (see below)
2 teaspoons ground cumin
2 tablespoons chili powder
1 tablespoon apple cider vinegar
1 15-ounce can diced tomatoes
1 28-ounce can crushed tomatoes
1 15-ounce can kidney beans, drained and rinsed
½ cup water for deglazing, plus 1 cup

Garnishes (optional)
Sharp cheddar cheese
Sour cream
Cilantro
Avocado
Sliced black olives

How to Make Bouquet Garni
Tie up the three sprigs of fresh parsley, one of fresh thyme, and one fresh bay leaf (and any other herbs) into a small bunch. Remove just before serving.

Directions

Prepare a coal fire for Dutch oven cooking at 325°F (see chart, page 23). Heat a 12-inch Dutch oven over ready coals, and when the pot is hot, add bison and brown it, stirring often for 5 minutes.

Add onion and carrot, and cook until both begin to soften, about 5 minutes. Add ½ cup of water to deglaze the pan, scraping brown bits from the bottom of the pan as the water evaporates. Add cauliflower, red bell pepper, garlic, and bouquet garni and cook until vegetables begin to soften, about 5 minutes.

Add cumin, chili powder, vinegar, tomatoes, and beans along with 1 cup of water. Bring to a boil; reduce to a simmer, cover and cook, stirring occasionally, until vegetables are fork tender, about 30-45 minutes. Serve with garnishes of choice.

Tip: Using fresh herbs for the bouquet garni is great, but dried herbs are also successful. Use 1 heaping tablespoon dried parsley, 1 teaspoon dried thyme or lemon thyme, and a single dried bay leaf. Tie up the dried herbs in a small bag sewn of muslin. Or grind the parsley and thyme and add to the dish. Add the bay leaf whole and remove before serving.

⋙ Braised Short Ribs ⋘
(DO)

Serves 4

Ingredients
16 bone-in beef chuck short ribs
4 tablespoons olive oil
3 large leeks, sliced into rounds
2 cups plus 3 tablespoons mango or apricot nectar (canned)
½ cup tequila
½ cup beef broth
3 to 4 tablespoons chipotle pepper puree (found in imported food section of most grocery stores)
Salt and pepper to taste

Directions
Prepare charcoal for Dutch oven temperature of 350°F (see chart, page 23). Add olive oil to heated Dutch oven, and when oil is hot, add the short ribs in batches, a few at a time, to cover the bottom of oven. Brown on all sides. When browned, remove to a platter and drain.

Add the leeks and brown about 5 minutes. Place short ribs back into Dutch oven and pour mango or apricot nectar, tequila, broth, and chipotle puree over ribs. Add salt and pepper.

Place lid on Dutch oven and braise for 2 to 3 hours. Remember that once you take the Dutch oven off of the heat, it will continue to cook what's inside. In this case, that is a good thing. This dish is wonderful as leftovers.

⮕ Butterflied Leg of Lamb à l'Orange ⬅
(TG)

Serves 4–6

Ingredients
1 cup fresh orange juice
¼ cup honey
¼ cup soy sauce
4 tablespoon fresh mint, chopped
1 tablespoon fresh ginger, chopped
5½ pounds butterflied leg of lamb
3 garlic cloves
1 teaspoon salt
Pepper to taste

Directions
For the marinade: Combine orange juice, soy sauce, honey, mint, and ginger. Mix well.

For the lamb: With a small sharp knife, cut openings evenly spaced in the skin of the meat and insert a sliver of garlic in each cut. Set lamb in a container and pour marinade over it. Place orange halves on both sides of the meat. Marinate 2 hours or longer, basting often. Remove lamb from the marinade and wipe dry. Salt and pepper to taste. Reserve marinade.

Place lamb on the Tuscan grill over ready coals. Grill about 6 to 15 minutes per side, depending on how you like your meat and how thick the lamb is. Baste often. If the meat starts to char before it's done, move it to indirect heat to finish cooking. Let rest for a few minutes before slicing and serving.

Tip: Because of the unevenness of the butterflied leg, you should have pieces that are perfectly done for everyone!

➤ Filet Mignon with Red Wine Reduction Sauce ➤ (TG)

Serves 2

Ingredients
2 filet mignon, preferably prime
Red Wine Reduction Sauce (page 196)

Directions
Build a fire and when hot break it down to coals. Place Tuscan grill over coals and let it heat up. Fire is ready when you can hold your hand 5 inches above grill only 2 to 4 seconds.

Place steaks on the grill and cook 4 minutes, then give them a quarter turn, keeping them on the same side. Cook 4 minutes more, then flip them over. Cook another 5 minutes, give them a quarter turn, and cook an additional 4 minutes for medium rare. If meat begins to char, move steaks off of direct heat.

Place steaks in foil and keep warm, letting meat rest for several minutes. Place steaks on individual plates and pour sauce around steak. Season with salt and pepper to taste.

❧ French Rabbit Stew with Baby Potatoes ❧
(DO)

Serves 2–3

Ingredients

3 slices bacon, cut in thirds

1½ cups onions, sliced

2 large cloves garlic, crushed

1 rabbit cut into 6 to 8 pieces

3 tablespoons flour

12 button mushrooms

2 cups chicken or beef broth

½ cup dry red or white wine

Thyme, parsley, bay leaf

8 to 10 baby potatoes, skin on

Directions

Prepare a coal fire for Dutch oven cooking at 350°F (see chart, page 23). When coals are ready, place the required amount under Dutch oven and fry bacon in Dutch oven until done. Cook onion and garlic in bacon drippings until transparent. Add rabbit pieces and sauté until golden. Sprinkle with flour and continue to brown rabbit another 5 minutes or so. Add mushrooms and cook for 2 minutes. Then add chicken or beef broth, red or white wine, thyme, parsley, and bay leaves. If you're using chicken broth, add white wine. If you've got beef broth, then red wine works well.

Place lid on Dutch oven and add required number of coals to the lid. Simmer 30 minutes and check for doneness, adding more broth if needed. In a separate fry pan on your cook stove, add oil and pan fry baby potatoes until skin is browned. Add potatoes to the rabbit in the Dutch oven about halfway through the cooking process.

Tip: If the sauce is too thin by the time the rabbit is done, make a roux to thicken it.

Variation: Skip the potatoes and boil up a package of fettuccine. The sauce in the Dutch oven is yummy with both.

❧ Grilled Rack of Lamb ❧
(TG)

This is a recipe you'll be able to get ready quickly, so you can spend more time stargazing. Be sure to marinate the rack of lamb at home, the night before your camping trip.

Serves 2–3

Ingredients
1 8-rib rack of New Zealand lamb
¼ cup olive oil
4 cloves garlic, pressed
½ Meyer lemon, juice and zest
3 tablespoons Dijon mustard
2 6-inch sprigs of fresh rosemary
½ teaspoon salt
½ teaspoon pepper

Directions

Make ahead: Dry off rack of lamb and place in a large resealable bag. In a measuring cup, add olive oil, garlic, lemon juice and zest, mustard, and salt and pepper. Snip rosemary leaves with sharp scissors into tiny pieces or mince with a knife. Add to measuring cup. Stir all ingredients together briskly with a fork until you have a thick, emulsified sauce. Pour into resealable bag over lamb. Refrigerate until ready to transfer to cooler.

At the campsite: Remove lamb from cooler and bring to forest temperature. (We would usually say room temperature, but come on! You're in the woods!) Start a wood fire and when coals have formed, knock the fire down and spread coals to form a nice coal bed. Set Tuscan grill over firepit and coals. Let the grill heat up until you can hold your hand over it for only 2 to 4 seconds.

Place the lamb on the grill bone side down and cook for 15 minutes, then turn it over and cook on meat side for another 15 minutes. We feel the only way to serve lamb is medium rare, pink in the middle. But if you like it cooked more than that, flip it a third time, back on to the bone side and cook for another 10 minutes.

When done, place the meat on a platter and let it rest for 10 minutes. Then slice down between each rib and serve, usually 3 to 4 ribs per person.

Tip: This is delicious served with boiled peewee potatoes that are tossed in melted butter and minced parsley, or over our Mascarpone Polenta with Wild Mushrooms (page 184).

⋙ Lamb Shank and Quince Tagine ⋘
(DO)

This dish is adapted from a recipe out of Martha Stewart Living.

Serves 4

Ingredients
4 lamb shanks (1¼ pounds each)
Coarse salt and freshly ground pepper to taste
2 tablespoons extra virgin olive oil
2 medium onions, halved and thinly sliced
2 garlic cloves, peeled
1½ teaspoons ground ginger
1 teaspoon ground cinnamon
1 teaspoon ground coriander
½ teaspoon ground cumin
½ teaspoon cayenne pepper
9 cups water
¼ cup honey
1 cup fresh cilantro, coarsely chopped
½ teaspoon saffron threads
4 quinces (about 2 pounds total), peeled and quartered
2 tablespoons fresh lemon juice
3 tablespoons Marcona almonds, toasted
Cooked couscous (follow package directions)

Directions
Prepare coals for Dutch oven cooking at 350°F (see chart, page 23). Season lamb shanks with salt and pepper. Heat oil in Dutch oven. Working in batches, if necessary, brown lamb shanks on all sides, about 4 minutes per side. Transfer lamb shanks to a bowl. Add onions, garlic,

ginger, cinnamon, coriander, cumin, and cayenne to drippings in pot, and cook 4 minutes. Return lamb and any juices to pot, and add enough water to cover (about 5 cups). Add honey, ⅓ cup cilantro, and the saffron, and bring to a boil. Cover with lid and add coals to top of lid according to Dutch oven chart (page 23), and simmer gently until lamb is tender, about 2 hours.

Meanwhile, bring 4 cups water to a boil. Add quinces and lemon juice. Cover. Reduce heat and simmer gently until tender but not falling apart, about 40 minutes. Drain, and then remove cores. Transfer half the quinces to a cutting board and mash with a fork.

Place lamb on a plate. Raise heat to medium-high, and simmer to reduce liquid by half, about 20 minutes, skimming fat. Return lamb to pot, and add whole and pureed quinces. Cook until sauce has thickened, 20 to 25 minutes.

To serve, season tagine with salt and pepper. Spoon couscous into bowls, top with one lamb shank, a few pieces of quince, and some sauce, then sprinkle with cilantro and almonds.

Variation: If you can't find quinces, which are only available in the fall, add ½ cup dried prunes and ½ cup dried apricots to the Dutch oven in the last 25 minutes of cooking.

➣ Neecie's BBQ Pork Ribs ➣
(TG)

Serves 3

Ingredients
1 rack St. Louis-style or baby back pork ribs
¼ cup Herbes de Provence
3 cloves garlic, pressed
Salt and pepper
Heavy duty aluminum foil
1 bottle of KC Masterpiece Hickory Brown Sugar Barbecue Sauce or your favorite

Directions
Cut two lengths of aluminum foil 4 inches longer on each end than slab of ribs. Place the rib rack on one piece of foil. Rub pressed garlic over ribs, then top with salt, pepper, and Herbes de Provence. Place second piece of foil over seasoned ribs and seal lengthwise along top and bottom. Fold in each end of foil, sealing well.

Place Tuscan grill over a medium-hot bed of coals in the firepit. Place foil packet of ribs on Tuscan grill, being careful not to tear foil. Cook for 1 hour.

Remove foil packet from grill and place on table. Carefully open packet. Hot steam will escape, so proceed with caution! There will be a lot of liquid in the packet. Discard the liquid. Ribs should be almost falling off the bone.

Bring your fire back up to medium hot. Sauce the ribs and place on Tuscan grill, turning ribs twice and saucing each turn. Ribs are done when sauce has formed a lovely glazed coating.

⇒ Rib Eye Steaks with Béarnaise Sauce ⇐
(TG)

Both the Béarnaise Sauce and Béarnaise Butter can be made at home and transported in your cooler to the campsite.

Serves 2

Ingredients
2 bone-in rib eye steaks (preferably prime)
Olive oil for rubbing on steaks
Béarnaise Sauce (page 188)

Directions
Build a fire and when hot, break it down to coals. Place Tuscan grill over the coals and let warm up. Fire is ready when you can hold your hand 5 inches above grill only 2 to 4 seconds. Rub each steak with olive oil, place steaks on the grill and cook 4 minutes, then give them a quarter turn, keeping them on the same side. Cook 4 minutes more, then flip them over. Cook another 4 minutes, give them a quarter turn, and cook an additional 4 minutes for medium rare. Place steaks in foil and keep warm, letting meat rest for several minutes. Plate the steaks and serve with Béarnaise sauce.

Variation: Instead of Béarnaise Sauce, spread thin slices of Béarnaise Butter (page 188) on the steaks before serving.

⇜ Sarah's Durban Lamb Curry ⇝
(W)

The smell of spices of the Indian markets in central Durban led Sarah Collins, founder of the Wonderbag, to come up with this delicious Wonderbag lamb curry.

Ingredients

2 tablespoons sunflower oil
2½ pounds lamb chops on bone (we prefer shoulder cut chops ideal for slow cooking and producing melt-in-the-mouth results)
1 medium onion, chopped
4 chilies, chopped
2 cloves garlic, diced
2 fresh ginger, crushed
3 tablespoons mild or medium curry powder
Salt and pepper to taste

1 28-ounce can tomatoes, chopped, peeled
1 cup water
1 bay leaf
1 14-ounce can baby lima beans, drained (also known as butter beans)
2 tablespoons tomato paste
½ cup cucumber, peeled and grated
1 cup plain yogurt
2 bananas, sliced
4 cups cooked white rice

Directions

Brown lamb in 2 tablespoons of oil, 2 minutes on each side and set aside. Brown the onions, and then add the chilies, garlic, ginger, and curry powder. Sauté for 2 minutes. Add the lamb back into the pot and stir, season with salt and pepper. Add peeled tomatoes and 1 cup of water and bring to a boil for 5 minutes.

Add bay leaf, lima beans, and tomato paste, stir, and allow to boil slowly for 15 minutes. Place lidded pot into the Wonderbag for 4 to 5 hours.

Combine grated cucumber and yogurt in a small bowl; stir to combine. Serve curry over rice with yogurt mixture and chopped bananas as toppings.

Tip: Add carrots or potatoes to this curry for extra texture and flavor.

⇌ Seyburn's Barbecued Tandoori Pork Loin with Jajik ⇌
(TG)

Serves 3–4

Ingredients

1½ pound pork tenderloin

⅓ cup plain yogurt

5 to 6 cloves garlic, minced

1 tablespoon freshly grated ginger

2 tablespoons lemon juice

2 teaspoons ground cumin

2 teaspoons ground coriander

1 teaspoon ground turmeric

1 teaspoon cayenne pepper

½ teaspoon ground cinnamon

Make ahead: Jajik (page 194)

Directions

Place pork loin in a sealable container. Mix next 9 ingredients together and coat the meat. Marinate in ice chest for as long as possible. Build a fire and when hot, break it down to coals. Place Tuscan grill over coals and let it heat up. Fire is ready when you can hold your hand 5 inches above grill only 2 to 4 seconds. Grill all 4 sides of tenderloin for 3 to 4 minutes each. When still pink, remove from heat. Let rest in foil 5 to 10 minutes.

Variation: Pork au Vin (another great marinade when grilling pork tenderloin)

Ingredients

¼ cup white wine

2 tablespoons olive oil

1 to 3 teaspoons of Herbes de Provence

Few dashes of soy sauce

2 tablespoons chopped shallots

1 teaspoon Wondra or flour

Directions

Place pork in a narrow dish and add all ingredients. Let sit for 1 to 2 hours. Reserve marinade and heat in saucepan to reduce. Stir in a little Wondra or flour to thicken and continue to simmer until thickened. Serve with pork and Jajik (page 194).

⊜ South African Beef Curry ⊜
(W)

Serves 6–8

Ingredients

3 pounds boned, fat-trimmed beef chuck
1 cup flour
¼ cup olive oil, or more as needed
2 onions (1 pound total), peeled and chopped
¼ cup mild or medium curry powder
2 tablespoons mustard seed
1 tablespoon minced garlic
1 teaspoon ground dried turmeric
2 cups beef broth
1 28-ounce can chopped tomatoes

2 tablespoons minced fresh jalapeño chilies
2 tablespoons minced fresh ginger, or 1 tablespoon ginger juice
1 firm-ripe banana (about 5 oz), peeled and thinly sliced
About ½ cup mango chutney (preferably Stonewall Kitchen brand)
About ⅓ cup shredded dried coconut, sweetened or unsweetened
Cucumber Yogurt Raita (page 191)

Directions

Rinse beef, pat dry, and cut into 1½-inch chunks. Roll in flour and sauté in olive oil in a heavy 5 to 6 quart pot until browned on all sides, about 5 to 10 minutes. This may be done in batches. Remove from pot, set aside. Add onions and sauté until softened, about 5 minutes.

Add to pot the curry powder, mustard seed, garlic, and turmeric; stir until spices are more fragrant, about 1 minute. Return browned beef to pot. Add broth, tomatoes, chilies, and ginger; stir to free browned bits. Return to a boil, cover, and simmer 15 to 20 minutes. Transfer pot to Wonderbag and let it "slow cook" for 4½ hours. Open Wonderbag and remove pot. If needed, heat up on your camp stove. Put banana, chutney, coconut, and Cucumber Yogurt Raita (page 191) each in separate small bowls. Ladle beef curry over rice on plates. Add banana, chutney, coconut, cucumber yogurt raita, and salt to taste.

Tip: A cast iron or heavy metal pot works best. We brought along our Le Creuset pot for this Wonderbag recipe and it worked out great! But Sarah Collins, founder of the Wonderbag, says any pot will do.

⋙ Spiced Lamb Burger with Harissa Mayo ⋘
(TG or V)

Makes 4 large or 6 small patties

Ingredients
2½ pounds ground lamb, preferably shoulder
1 medium onion, very finely chopped
¾ cup fresh flat-leaf parsley, chopped
1 tablespoon ground coriander
¾ teaspoon ground cumin
½ teaspoon ground cinnamon
2 teaspoons kosher salt
1½ teaspoon freshly ground black pepper
¼ cup olive oil, plus more for grilling
Pita bread or whole wheat buns
Harissa Mayonnaise (page 193)

Directions
Using a fork, mix lamb, onion, parsley, coriander, cumin, cinnamon, salt, pepper, and ¼ cup oil in a large bowl. Cover and chill at least 1 hour. Prepare fire for medium heat. Oil Tuscan grill and place over coals. Form lamb mixture into patties and grill about 5 minutes per side. Serve with harissa mayonnaise.

☞ Cast Iron Ratatouille ☜
(DO or V)

Serves 6

Ingredients

4 tablespoons olive oil
2 garlic cloves, minced
3 sprigs thyme, leaves only
1 Vidalia sweet onion, thinly sliced
Herbes de Provence
Fleur de sel (French sea salt), or substitute any good quality sea salt
Freshly cracked black pepper

3 to 4 Roma tomatoes, sliced very thinly
2 yellow or green zucchini, sliced very thinly
2 to 3 long, narrow eggplant (try Japanese or any that have a longer shape), sliced very thinly
1 small log good quality goat cheese
½ cup fresh basil, chopped

Directions

Prepare a coal fire for Dutch oven cooking at 325°F (see chart, page 23). In your Dutch oven, warm 1 tablespoon olive oil and cook garlic and thyme for 1 minute over medium heat or until fragrant. Transfer to a large mixing bowl and set aside. Add another tablespoon of olive oil to the oven and caramelize onions, seasoned with cracked black pepper and fleur de sel over medium heat, about 15 minutes. Remove from heat and spread onions evenly across the bottom of the Dutch oven or cast iron skillet. Prep veggies for arrangement. Pat dry and salt tomato slices with fleur de sel. Set aside. Add zucchini and eggplant slices to bowl with garlic and thyme. Toss with 2 more tablespoons of olive oil and season with fleur de sel and cracked pepper. Arrange the vegetable slices in a spiral around the Dutch oven, working from the outside in. Stack zucchini, eggplant, and tomato in the same order until a complete circle is formed. Once the outside circle is complete, begin another just inside. Continue until the spiral is finished and the middle is closed. Crumble goat cheese over all. Place Dutch oven back over the coals, cover with lid, and place six coals around the edge of the lid. Cook until the vegetables are browned and tender, about 15 minutes. Allow to rest for 5 minutes before serving. Add chopped fresh basil to top and serve.

Variation: You can prepare this dish in a cast iron fry pan and cook it over a Volcano grill, set up with a single row of coals in the bottom. Remove the grill from the unit and place the fry pan on top of the unit. Cover with the heatproof lid and cook as above.

⋙ Eggplant Parmesan ⋘
(TG or V)

Have you ever been camping when you didn't want to spend a lot of time preparing the first night's meal? Well, the solution to that is easy. Simply prepare a one-dish meal ahead of time at home and then reheat at the campground. Eggplant Parmesan is a perfect make-ahead meal.

Serves 6

Ingredients

2½ pounds Japanese eggplant cut a generous ⅓-inch thick, lengthwise
½ cup olive oil, plus 3 tablespoons
1 large yellow onion, coarsely chopped
3 cloves garlic, coarsely chopped, plus 2 cloves minced
½ teaspoon red pepper flakes
3 roasted red peppers from jar (Mezzetta brand or other)
2 28-ounce cans plum tomatoes and their juices, crushed with your hands
1 28-ounce can crushed tomatoes
3 tablespoons freshly chopped Italian parsley
3 tablespoons freshly chopped basil, plus freshly torn leaves
1 tablespoon freshly chopped oregano
12 ounces grated smoked mozzarella and ½ pound fresh mozzarella, thinly sliced
12 ounces grated fontina
¼ cup grated Pecorino Romano
½ cup panko breadcrumbs
¼ cup grated Parmesan
Salt and pepper, to taste

Directions

Make ahead: Preheat oven to 450°F. Line a rimmed baking sheet with parchment and brush the parchment with olive oil. Arrange eggplant slices in a single layer on the baking sheet. You may need more than one baking sheet. Brush eggplant with olive oil and sprinkle with salt. Flip the slices over and repeat. Roast until golden brown, about 30 to 40 minutes, flipping the eggplant halfway through. In the meantime, prepare the sauce. Heat 3 tablespoons oil in a heavy pot over medium-high heat. Add the onion and cook until soft. Add the garlic and red pepper flakes and cook for 1 minute. Add the red peppers and cook for 1 minute. Add tomatoes, bring to a boil, and cook, stirring occasionally, until thickened, about 25 to 30 minutes. Let cool for a bit and then transfer the mixture to a food processor and process until smooth. Return the mixture back to the pot, add the parsley, basil, and oregano. Cook for 10 minutes longer. Cover the bottom of a buttered 9 x 13 baking dish with some of the tomato sauce and arrange half of the eggplant over the sauce. Cover the eggplant with some of the sauce, grated mozzarella, fontina, Pecorino Romano, and some of the torn basil leaves. Repeat to make 3 layers ending with the sauce. Top with the fresh mozzarella and remaining Pecorino Romano. Cover with foil and refrigerate.
Make the final topping by combining 2 tablespoons of olive oil, 2 teaspoons minced garlic, ¼ cup of Parmesan, and ½ cup panko in a small bowl. Cover and refrigerate.

At the campsite: Prepare a fire for medium-high heat. Take the covered eggplant dish and topping out of the cooler. Keep the eggplant covered and heat on Tuscan grill or Volcano over fire until bubbling. Remove foil and sprinkle panko mixture evenly over the top. Place a heatproof hood over the casserole. Cook until topping is golden brown.

Tip: Save time and use a jar of your favorite marinara sauce instead of making the sauce from scratch.

Variation: If Japanese eggplants are not available, use regular eggplant cut into ⅓-inch rounds.

➤ Grilled Market Vegetables with Romesco Sauce ⭐
(TG or V)

Serves 4–6

Ingredients
1 pound green beans, trimmed
2 to 3 Yukon Gold potatoes, sliced lengthwise in ½-inch planks
2 medium-sized zucchini, sliced lengthwise in ½-inch planks
2 garlic cloves, pressed
1 cup cherry tomatoes, halved
1 bunch chives, cut in ½-inch lengths
2 tablespoons pine nuts
¼ cup black olives
¼ cup green olives
Salt and pepper
Romesco Sauce (page 196)

Directions
Prepare grill for medium heat. Combine green beans, potatoes, zucchini, and pressed garlic in a large bowl. Drizzle in some olive oil and season with salt and pepper. Toss to coat.

Grill potatoes on the cooler part of the grill 12 to 15 minutes, turning once, until tender.

Grill the green beans and zucchini on the hotter part of the grill 3 to 5 minutes, turning once, until tender.

While still warm, cut the vegetables into bite-sized pieces. Put all vegetables on a platter. Top with cherry tomatoes, olives, chives, and pine nuts. Spoon romesco sauce over the top of vegetables.

⤜ Marinated Tofu for Grilling ⤛
(TG, V, or CS)

Marinating tofu a day or two before your camping trip is a perfect make-ahead dish.

Serves 2–3

Ingredients

1 package of firm tofu
½ cup soy sauce or tamari
¾ cup water
½ cup white wine or mirin (sweet cooking sake)
⅓ cup sugar

¼ cup dark sesame oil
½ ounce dried shiitake mushrooms
1½ teaspoons dry mustard
2 tablespoons ginger, grated
4 garlic cloves, crushed

Directions

Make ahead: Slice block of tofu in half horizontally, place in colander and drain for 10 to 15 minutes. Prepare marinade by combining all ingredients in a small saucepan. Bring to a boil, then reduce the heat and simmer for 10 minutes. Place the tofu in a square or rectangular nonreactive pan. Pour the hot marinade over the tofu, being sure to cover it with the marinade. Cool, then cover with a lid or seal tightly with plastic and refrigerate for 24 hours. Transfer to cooler when leaving on your camping trip.

At the campsite: Prepare coals for grilling over medium heat, and lightly oil the grate. Grill the tofu 5 to 7 minutes each side until almost blackened in spots, brushing occasionally with the marinade.

Variation: Instead of grilling, this recipe can serve as a morning breakfast scramble. Just add scallions, bell pepper, button mushrooms, and chopped tomato.

⇒ Mushroom Quesadillas ⇐
(CS)

Serves 2

Ingredients
4 whole wheat flour tortillas
8 ounces chanterelle mushrooms, chopped
8 ounces crimini mushrooms, chopped
1 onion sliced thinly, using mandoline
4 tablespoons butter, divided, plus some
½ teaspoon fresh or dried thyme
6 ounces good quality fontina cheese, sliced ¼-inch thick
Salt and pepper

Directions
Sauté mushrooms and thyme in 2 tablespoons butter until soft. Caramelize onion in remaining butter. Mix mushrooms and onions together. Add salt and pepper. Place a small amount of butter in a fry pan and melt. Add one of the flour tortillas and strategically place a few cheese slices on it, not too close to the edges. Add mushroom/onion mixture and a couple more cheese slices. Top with another flour tortilla and gently press down with a spatula. Turn quesadilla over and cook until nicely browned. Cut into wedges and serve warm.

Variation: If chanterelles are not available, you can substitute shiitakes or maitakes (in Japan known as "the dancing mushroom"). Fresh versions of these mushrooms can be found at many farmers markets.

⥸ Portobello Mushroom Burger ⥷
(CS, TG)

Serves 2

Ingredients

⅛ cup olive oil plus 2 tablespoons
1 tablespoon balsamic vinegar
Pinch smoked salt
2 large portobello mushrooms
1 medium onion, sliced thinly
2 cups assorted mushrooms (cremini,
chanterelle, shiitake), chopped
1 garlic clove, pressed

1 teaspoon fresh thyme leaves
2 tablespoons butter
1 tablespoon snipped chives
2 ounces good quality blue cheese
2 brioche or hamburger buns, toasted
Smoky barbecue aioli, preferably Stonewall
Kitchen brand

Directions

Mix together olive oil, vinegar, and smoked salt. Marinate portobello mushrooms for 30 minutes. Reserve marinade. Prepare grill for medium heat. In a fry pan, caramelize onion in 2 tablespoons olive oil, about 30 minutes, stirring often. In a separate fry pan, sauté assorted mushrooms, pressed garlic, and fresh thyme in butter for 5 minutes. Add snipped fresh chives and set aside. Place Tuscan grill over medium-hot coals. Put marinated mushrooms on grill gill side down and cook until liquid releases, about 5 minutes. Turn and baste with marinade. Grill another 5 minutes. Turn again with gill side up. Combine sautéed mushroom mixture with blue cheese. Carefully stuff mixture into portobello mushrooms. Cover with heatproof lid or foil and let cheese melt. Carefully remove portobellos from the grill and place on bottom half of bun. Top with caramelized onions. Spread top half of bun with a smoky barbecue aioli or whatever condiment you have on hand.

Variation: To make a lunch salad, place mushrooms on a bed of quinoa tossed with bits of dried fruit, chopped parsley, a teaspoon of orange zest, and mustard vinaigrette. Or use smaller portobellos and serve as an appetizer.

⮞ Portobello Penne Pasta Casserole ⮜
(TG)

This dish is another one that you can make at home before you leave on your camping trip. It's almost as easy as opening a package of weenies and cracking a can of beans, but way more delicious!

Serves 8

Ingredients
1 8-ounce package uncooked penne pasta
2 tablespoons olive oil
½ pound portobello mushrooms, thinly sliced
½ onion, chopped
½ cup butter
¼ cup all-purpose flour
1 large clove garlic, minced

½ teaspoon dried thyme
2 cups milk
2 cups shredded mozzarella cheese
1 10-ounce package frozen chopped spinach, thawed
¼ cup soy sauce

Directions
Preheat oven to 350°F. Lightly grease a 9 x 13-inch stainless steel baking dish.

Bring a large pot of lightly salted water to a boil. Place pasta in the pot, cook for 8 to 10 minutes, until al dente, and then drain.

Heat the oil in a saucepan over medium heat. Stir in the mushrooms and onions, cook 2 minutes and then set aside. Melt butter in the saucepan. Mix in flour, garlic, and thyme. Gradually mix in milk until thickened. Stir in 1 cup cheese until melted. Remove saucepan from heat, and mix in cooked pasta, mushrooms, spinach, and soy sauce. Transfer to the prepared baking dish, and top with remaining cheese.

Bake 20 minutes in the preheated oven until bubbly and lightly brown. Remove from oven and bring to room temperature. Cover with foil and transport to campsite. Warm it up by placing Tuscan grill over wood fire in firepit and placing stainless steel baking dish, still covered with foil, on grill until heated through.

➤ Ravioli al Pomodoro Fresco ➤
(CS)

Buitoni's Mushroom Agnolotti is a rich pasta filled with fresh cheeses, mushrooms, and roasted garlic.

Serves 2

Ingredients
1 package Buitoni Mushroom Agnolotti (you can substitute sausage ravioli)
¼ cup olive oil
2 to 3 cloves garlic, minced or pressed
6 Roma tomatoes, chopped
2 tablespoons capers
4 green onions, sliced
¼ cup white wine
1 tablespoon butter
Salt and pepper
Handful of fresh basil, chopped

Directions
Get a pot of salted water going to a low boil. Boil agnolotti per package instructions.

Meanwhile, heat olive oil slowly in a sauté pan. Add garlic and sauté about 1 minute. Then add tomatoes, capers, and onions. Cook for about 2 minutes before adding a splash or two of white wine. Reduce sauce for about 4 minutes.

Turn off heat. Add butter and fresh basil. Pour sauce over ravioli. Add Parmesan, salt, and pepper to taste.

➤ Tagine of Butternut Squash, Shallots, Carrots, and Prunes ➤ (DO)

Serves 4–6

Ingredients
2 to 3 tablespoons olive oil with a pat of butter
1 to 1½-inch piece of fresh ginger, peeled and finely chopped or grated
1 to 2 cinnamon sticks or 1 to 2 teaspoons of ground cinnamon
16 small shallots, peeled and left whole
1 medium-sized butternut squash, peeled and cut into bite-sized chunks
2 medium carrots, peeled and cut into bite-sized chunks
1 cup pitted prunes
1 tablespoon dark honey
2 cups vegetable stock
1 small bunch of cilantro leaves, roughly chopped
1 small bunch of fresh mint leaves, chopped
Sea salt and freshly ground pepper

Directions
Prepare your firepit for Dutch oven cooking at 350°F (see chart, page 23). Heat the olive oil and butter in Dutch oven. Stir in ginger and cinnamon sticks. Toss in the shallots. When they begin to color, add squash and carrots. Sauté for 2 to 3 minutes, then add the prunes and the honey. Pour in vegetable stock and bring to a boil. Reduce heat under Dutch oven, cover with lid, add required number of coals to lid, and cook gently for about 25 minutes.

Remove the lid and stir in some of the cilantro and mint. Season to taste with salt and pepper. Reduce the liquid, if necessary, by cooking for another 2 to 3 minutes without the lid. The vegetables should be tender and slightly caramelized and the sauce very syrupy. Sprinkle with remaining cilantro and mint and serve immediately.

≳ Veggie Skewers ≲
(TG)

Serves 4

Ingredients

½ cup soy sauce

¼ cup melted butter

1 clove garlic, pressed

Salt and pepper

2 bell peppers, one red and one yellow, cut into 1-inch pieces

12 button mushrooms

8 slices of Yvonne's Marinated Japanese Eggplants (page 177)

1 yellow onion, cut into 1-inch pieces

1 basket of cherry tomatoes

2 zucchini, cut into rounds ½-inch thick

4 bamboo skewers, soaked in water 1 hour or longer

Directions

For the basting sauce: Combine soy sauce, melted butter, garlic, salt, and pepper in a bowl and set aside.

For the skewers: Assemble by starting with a piece of bell pepper. This keeps the rest of the veggies from falling off. Then skewer one end of a slice of marinated eggplant, leaving the rest to weave in between the following veggies. Alternate one mushroom, one piece of onion, one cherry tomato, and one piece of zucchini, then repeat, weaving in the eggplant at random. End with another piece of bell pepper.

Place finished skewers on a platter and baste with basting sauce. Set your Tuscan grill over a medium fire. You can either place the skewers directly onto the Tuscan grill or place them in a grill basket, if you have one. (This makes them really easy to turn.) Grill the skewers until charred, turn them over and baste them, then repeat, basting at each turn. Cook to desired doneness, 5 minutes total for crispy texture. Serve hot over rice, quinoa, or peewee potatoes.

Savory Sides

Hopefully you've heeded our warnings from Tips and Tricks (page 21) regarding the proximity of your greens to freezing temperatures. If not, well, you might as well skip right over the salads because your greens have likely been rendered a flaccid mess. If you've made it this far in your camping life, to the point of being able to successfully drive yourself to a campground and consider cooking a gourmet meal, you're also likely to know exactly how useless a flaccid mess can be. However, if you were patient enough to read through the beginning of this book, then get ready for some wholesome stiff greens.

Of course not all salads have greens. Keep an eye out for the Tomato, Feta, and Watermelon Salad with Mint (page 166), perfectly refreshing on a hot summer day. Heartier sides like our Coal-Roasted Eggplants (page 170) and Mascarpone Polenta with Wild Mushrooms (page 184) are fantastically warming for the cooler days.

⇒ Caprese Salad ⇐

Serves 4

Ingredients
Fresh arugula
2 ripe red tomatoes, sliced in rounds
2 ripe yellow tomatoes, sliced in rounds
2 ripe Green Zebra tomatoes, sliced in rounds (an heirloom variety available seasonally)
2 balls of fresh buffalo mozzarella (made from water buffalo milk), sliced in rounds and then cut in half
1 large handful fresh basil, chopped
6 snipped fresh chives
4 tablespoons olive oil
2 tablespoons balsamic vinegar or balsamic glaze

Directions
Assemble salad as follows: Begin with a bed of arugula on a platter. Then, working in concentric circles or rows, start with laying a red tomato slice on top of arugula, a slice of mozzarella, a yellow tomato slice, another slice of mozzarella, then another green tomato slice, continuing in this fashion around the platter, overlapping each time, until all tomatoes and cheese have been used.

Sprinkle chopped basil in a narrow line on top of each row of tomatoes and cheese. Sprinkle all around with fresh chives. Drizzle olive oil and balsamic over all. Serve with crispy French bread rounds, slightly toasted and rubbed with a cut garlic clove.

Tip: We also like to sprinkle the top of this dish with thinly sliced orange cherry tomatoes for even more color. Beautiful!

⋙ Chopped Kale and Arugula Salad ⋘

Serves 6

Ingredients
1 bag of baby kale or 1 bunch red Russian kale
1 bag of baby arugula
1 ripe Haas avocado, diced
10 fresh chives, snipped
1 wedge of Greek feta cheese
1 lemon, juice and zest
¼ cup olive oil
Salt and pepper to taste

Directions
Combine kale and arugula on a chopping board and chop together until pieces are small. Place in a bowl along with avocado, crumbled feta to taste, and chives. Mix well. Squeeze the juice of one fresh lemon over the salad, and add the zest. Sprinkle with olive oil, salt and pepper, and serve.

⇒ Grilled Caesar Salad ⇐
(TG)

The make-ahead yummy Caesar salad dressing below makes all the difference in this recipe. Feel free to use a bottled version, but homemade is incredibly easy to make and tastes so much better than store bought.

Serves 4–6

Ingredients
3 heads romaine hearts, halved lengthwise
Salt and freshly ground pepper

Freshly grated Parmesan
Caesar Salad Dressing

Make ahead: Caesar Salad Dressing
Ingredients
2 soft boiled eggs
2 cloves garlic
1 can of anchovies in oil
2 teaspoons Dijon
¼ cup fresh lemon juice

⅓ cup red wine or tarragon vinegar
¾ cup olive oil
1 teaspoon salt
Fresh pepper to taste
Freshly grated Parmesan

Directions
Place all ingredients except olive oil into a blender and pulse a few times. With the blender running, pour the olive oil in slowly for the dressing to emulsify. Store in a container and place in fridge until ready to transfer to cooler. Shake well before dressing the salad.

At the campsite: Brush romaine hearts with olive oil. Place on Tuscan grill over medium heat and let grill for 2 minutes, turning with tongs as grill marks appear. Do not over-wilt the lettuce. Remove lettuce to a cutting board and cut into 2-inch wide strips. Place in a bowl and drizzle with the dressing. Toss well to coat.

Variation: For a twist on this classic, substitute Parmesan with crumbled blue cheese.

≥ Grilled Peach and Prosciutto Salad ≤
(TG)

Make the vinaigrette ahead of time. "Prep in the kitchen and place in the cooler" will soon become your camping motto!

Serves 4

Ingredients

4 large or 6 to 8 small firm-ripe peaches, cut into sixths

1 bunch basil, leaves left intact

1 bunch chives, finely chopped (We do this with scissors.)

8 ounces arugula (1 bag)

8 slices prosciutto, pulled apart into small shreds

Salt and pepper to taste

Tomato Vinaigrette

Make ahead: Tomato Vinaigrette
Ingredients

2 tablespoons olive oil

1 tablespoon vinegar

2 small ripe heirloom tomatoes, stems removed and cut into quarters

Juice and zest of 1 lemon

Juice and zest of 1 lime

Salt and pepper

Directions

Place all of the ingredients into a blender and whizz together for 30 seconds so that you have a smooth emulsion. Pour into a tightly sealed container and refrigerate until time to transfer to cooler.

At the campsite: Place all greens in a large bowl. Put peach slices in another bowl with a bit of olive oil, and toss to coat. Sprinkle salt and pepper over peaches. Place Tuscan grill over a medium fire. Place peaches on the grill and cook for 90 seconds. Carefully turn the peaches and cook again for 1 minute. Carefully remove the peaches from the grill and add them to the salad. Gently toss so that the peaches stay intact. Serve immediately. Peaches should still be warm.

⋑ Pear and Fennel Salad ⋐

Serves 4

Ingredients
2 ripe, but still a little firm, pears, sliced ⅛-inch thick
1 fennel bulb, sliced paper thin, using mandoline
1 teaspoon olive oil
Squeeze of lemon
Handful of baby romaine and radicchio or other salad greens
¼ cup toasted walnuts
¼ cup crumbled blue cheese
Chopped parsley

Dressing
¼ cup olive oil
1 tablespoon sherry wine vinegar
1 teaspoon Dijon mustard
¼ teaspoon honey
Salt and pepper to taste

Directions
Drizzle olive oil and a squeeze of lemon over sliced fennel. Sprinkle with salt. Toss and set aside.

Divide salad greens and place in 4 individual bowls. Whisk together ingredients for dressing. Toss together pears and fennel with dressing and divide between the bowls. Top each bowl with blue cheese, toasted walnuts, and chopped parsley.

⇒ Potato Salad ⇐

This is an easy make-ahead-at-home recipe. It will give you more time to put up your hammock and relax when you arrive at the campground.

Serves 4

Ingredients

1½ pounds small red, purple, white, or yellow potatoes, scrubbed but left whole
2 hardboiled eggs, chopped
1 to 2 carrots, thinly sliced
1 to 2 radishes, thinly sliced

2 to 3 green onions, thinly sliced
A handful of Italian flat-leaf parsley, chervil, dill, or any combination thereof, chopped
6 to 7 ounces of crème fraîche or sour cream
Salt and freshly ground pepper

Vinaigrette

½ cup olive oil
¼ cup champagne vinegar
1 tablespoon Dijon mustard

Directions

Whisk together all three ingredients and set aside.

Bring the potatoes to a boil in a large pot of water and simmer for approximately 20 minutes or until tender. Drain. Cut in half or quarters or, depending on how big your potatoes are, into manageable bite-sized pieces. Pour vinaigrette over warm potatoes and let cool.

Combine the potatoes with the eggs, carrots, radishes, green onions, and fresh herbs, mixing gently. Add enough crème fraîche or sour cream until the ingredients are coated lightly. If you want a more traditional creamy potato salad, you can add some homemade mayonnaise. Add the salt and pepper to taste. Let chill and then taste again, adjusting seasoning if necessary.

⋗ Quinoa Salad ⋖
(CS)

Serves 8

Ingredients
1 cup quinoa, rinsed
2 cups water
2 tablespoons olive oil
1 medium onion, finely chopped
1 small red bell pepper, finely chopped
½ pound fresh kale, leafy part pulled off of mid rib, chopped
½ pound baby bok choy, chopped
Salt and pepper to taste
⅓ cup hazelnuts, chopped
2 tablespoons chives, finely chopped
2 tablespoons parsley, finely chopped
2 tablespoons cilantro, finely chopped

Directions
Place the quinoa in a saucepan with the water and bring to a boil. Reduce to a simmer, cover, and cook until the quinoa has absorbed all the water. Pour olive oil into a large skillet over medium heat. Add the onion and bell pepper and cook until soft. Add the kale and bok choy and cook for 5 to 7 minutes. Vegetables should still be bright green. Add salt and pepper to taste. Add the cooked quinoa, chopped hazelnuts, and all of the herbs. Squeeze the juice of half a lemon over all and drizzle with olive oil. Mix together well and serve.

⋟ Tomato, Feta, and Watermelon Salad with Mint ⋞

Serves 4–6

Ingredients

1 small watermelon, seedless
1 teaspoon salt
1 cup crumbled feta cheese

1 cup fresh mint, julienned
4 to 6 large tomatoes (heirloom or other seasonal variety)

Directions

Cut watermelon into 1¼-inch cubes. Add salt and let stand while you prepare dressing. Add cheese and mint to the tomatoes and watermelon, then the dressing. Toss gently to combine.

Dressing

Ingredients

¼ cup fresh orange juice
1 to 2 lemons, squeezed
¼ cup minced shallots
1 tablespoon honey

½ cup extra virgin olive oil
½ teaspoon salt
Dash of sherry vinegar (optional)

Directions

Whisk all ingredients together except olive oil, and then slowly add oil, continuing to whisk.

Variation: Add a handful or two of baby arugula if you have it on hand. You can substitute shaved Parmesan for feta.

➤ Artichokes with Garlic Aioli ➤
(TG or V)

Serves 4

Ingredients

2 artichokes
1½ lemons
Salt and pepper
Olive oil

1 cup mayonnaise
2 garlic cloves
1 tablespoon snipped chives

Directions

Trim artichokes by slicing off the bottom stems, and cut artichokes in half. Bring a large pot of water to a boil. Add juice of one lemon and a pinch of salt. Lower heat and gently drop in the artichokes. Simmer for 20 minutes.

Prepare a grill for medium-high heat. Remove artichokes from water and drain. Drizzle olive oil on artichokes. Place artichokes on the grill cut side down. Continue to grill for 5 minutes per side until artichokes start to show grill marks and char, about 15 to 20 minutes. Cool and remove choke (the hairy part on the inside of the artichoke) with a teaspoon, they don't call it choke for nothin'! Serve with garlic aioli for dipping.

Garlic Aioli

Press garlic cloves into a small bowl. Squeeze half a lemon into the bowl. Add 1 cup of mayonnaise and snipped chives. Stir ingredients together.

Tip: Buy the 8-ounce jar of mayonnaise, then you can put the aioli back into the jar and store in your cooler for other uses, such as a sandwich spread or as a side for grilled fish.

Variation: Add freshly grated ginger and curry to the mayo. Omit chives.

⇒ Asparagus Wrapped with Smoked Salmon ⇐
(TG)

Serves 4–6

Ingredients
1 bunch of hefty asparagus (12-15 spears)
2 tablespoons olive oil
1 tablespoon fresh rosemary or other fresh herbs (chives, dill, or parsley)
Pinch of salt
Freshly ground pepper
6 ounces thinly sliced smoked salmon (1 slice per spear)

Directions
Prepare grill for medium heat. Peel lower third of asparagus spears with a potato peeler. Finely chop the rosemary. Drizzle asparagus with olive oil. Sprinkle with rosemary, salt, and pepper. Toss to coat. Place directly on the grill or in a grill basket. Grill until just tender and lightly charred, about 5 minutes. Once the asparagus have cooled, wrap each spear with a slice of smoked salmon.

Variation: Wrap asparagus with prosciutto or Speck Americano, an exceptional ham made by smoking prosciutto with applewood.

❧ Carrots with Cumin-Honey Vinaigrette ❧
(CS)

Serves 4

Ingredients

3 tablespoons olive oil
1 large onion, peeled and sliced into ¼-inch rounds
10 medium carrots, peeled and cut on an angle into ⅛-inch slices
24 whole Moroccan black olives, pitted

8 preserved lemon slices
Salt and freshly ground black pepper
Paprika
Cayenne pepper
1 teaspoon whole cumin seed, toasted (optional)

Directions

Heat 1 tablespoon olive oil in a large nonstick skillet over high heat. Add onion and sauté for about 3 minutes on each side, or until translucent. Remove from skillet, coarsely chop and set aside.

Heat remaining olive oil in the skillet over high heat. Add carrots and sauté for about 5 minutes or until well browned. Reduce heat to medium and cook carrots until tender, for about another 2 minutes. Add the onions, olives, and preserved lemon slices. Season with salt, pepper, paprika, and cayenne, to taste. Remove from heat and set aside.

Cumin-Honey Vinaigrette

Mix together 2 teaspoons honey, 2 tablespoons lemon juice, 1 teaspoon chopped fresh mint, and 2 teaspoons ground cumin. Slowly whisk in 4 tablespoons olive oil. Season with salt and pepper, to taste. Pour dressing over carrots and toss well. Sprinkle 1 teaspoon whole toasted cumin seed over top (optional).

Tip: If you don't have preserved lemons on hand, you can add a tablespoon of fresh orange zest (or a mixture of lemon and orange zest) and 1 tablespoon of orange juice.

⇒ Coal-Roasted Eggplants ⇐

This recipe is adapted from Bon Appétit.

Serves 4

Ingredients
2 small eggplants (about 1 pound total)

Directions
Prepare a hardwood-charcoal fire in a firepit. Let coals cool to medium heat (coals should be covered with ash and glowing red with no black remaining).

Place eggplants directly on coals and cook, turning occasionally, until skins are blackened and flesh has collapsed, 10 to 15 minutes. (Alternatively, grill on the grate of a gas or charcoal grill over medium-high heat, turning occasionally, 15 to 20 minutes.) Transfer to a rimmed baking sheet and let cool slightly.

Carefully remove skins from eggplants, leaving stems intact. Place eggplants on a wire rack set inside the same rimmed baking sheet and let stand 30 minutes to allow excess water to drain. Just before serving, split lengthwise and serve drizzled with extra virgin olive oil and some coarse salt.

Variation: Serve with a Smoky Tomato Sauce (page 197) or Yogurt and Sumac Sauce (page 197).

Corn on the Cob in the Husk
(TG)

Serves 4

Ingredients
4 ears of fresh corn on the cob, yellow or white, husks on
2 tablespoons fresh oregano, chopped
2 tablespoons fresh chives, snipped
4 tablespoons Parmesan cheese, freshly grated
4 tablespoons of mayonnaise or melted butter

Directions
Pull the silk off of each piece of corn and discard. You will have to pull down the husks to get it all, but leave the husks attached. Soak corn and husks in a large pan of water so the husks won't dry out and burn when you put them on the grill. (This also helps steam the corn inside.) Pat dry corn and husks with dishtowel and then spread mayonnaise or melted butter over corn with a basting brush. Sprinkle with herbs and Parmesan. Close husks over corn and tie off ends to make a packet with string or a rubber band. Cook on Tuscan grill over medium coals, turning frequently, until done. When ready to serve, pull back husks to form a handle and secure with a rubber band.

Variation: You can add cooked bacon, cayenne, smoked salt, Béarnaise Butter (page 188), or many other combinations. The sky's the limit when it comes to different topping possibilities. Use your imagination!

⋙ Grilled Fingerling Potatoes ⋘
(TG or V)

Serves 4–6

Ingredients

3 pounds fingerling potatoes, or any thin-skinned new potato

½ cup plus 2 tablespoons white wine

Olive oil for brushing

½ cup organic mayonnaise

1 tablespoon whole-grain mustard

2 tablespoons fresh flat-leaf parsley, minced

2 tablespoons fresh tarragon, minced

Salt and pepper to taste

Directions

Prepare grill for medium-high heat. Brush and oil the grill grate or a vegetable grill basket. Bring a pot three-fourths full of salted water to a boil over high heat on your camp stove. Add the potatoes and return to a boil. Cover, reduce the heat to medium-high, and parboil until the potatoes can be pierced with the tip of a knife but are not completely tender, about 10 minutes. Drain.

In a large bowl, combine the warm potatoes and ½ cup white wine and stir to coat. Let cool to room temperature, stirring often. Cut the potatoes in half lengthwise and brush with olive oil. In a small bowl, stir together mayonnaise, mustard, 2 tablespoons white wine, parsley, and tarragon. Let the dressing stand for 10 minutes.

Arrange the potatoes on the grill grate or in the basket directly over medium-high heat. Grill, turning once, until the potatoes are nicely grill-marked, about 5 minutes per side. Transfer the potatoes to a large bowl, add the dressing and stir to coat. Season with salt and pepper. Serve the potatoes immediately or cover tightly and place in cooler for about 1 hour and serve cold.

⤳ Haricots Verts with Shiitake Mushrooms and Pine Nuts ⤶
(CS)

Haricots verts are very thin, young beans that come in green and yellow. They look great together! If they are really tiny you don't have to pre-blanch them. If they are big, then boil three cups of water and add the beans for 3 minutes, or until bright green. Drain them, and then add to sautéed mushrooms in skillet.

Serves 4

Ingredients
¼ cup toasted pine nuts
2 tablespoons olive oil
¼ pound shiitake mushrooms, chopped
2 tablespoons fresh thyme leaves
1 garlic clove, pressed
½ pound French green beans, or ¼ pound green and ¼ pound yellow
½ cup fresh chives, snipped into small pieces
Salt and pepper to taste

Directions
Toast pine nuts in a small skillet over medium heat on your camp stove, tossing often, about 5 minutes. Set aside. Add olive oil to the skillet and add the shiitake mushrooms, thyme, and garlic. Sauté for 5 minutes, then add the beans. Cook until al dente. Do not overcook! Sprinkle chives over all and serve.

⇒ Maple-Roasted Brussels Sprouts on the Grill ⇐
(TG or V)

Serves 4-6

Ingredients
1 pound Brussels sprouts, as uniform in size as possible
1 tablespoon extra virgin olive oil
½ teaspoon sea salt
½ teaspoon ground black pepper
1 tablespoon maple syrup
2 tablespoons pine nuts

Directions
Prepare the grill for medium to medium-high heat.

Cut off the stem end of the Brussels sprouts and remove any outer yellowing leaves. Toss sprouts in olive oil.

Make a foil pouch. Place the Brussels sprouts in the center of the pouch and roll up the sides, leaving the top open. Sprinkle the sprouts with sea salt. Place the pouch on the grill and cover with lid. Stir after about 5 minutes. Let cook another 10 to 15 minutes.

Drizzle with maple syrup and toss with pine nuts.

Variation: Shelled sunflower seeds, raw pumpkin seeds, or walnuts pieces are a good substitute for pine nuts.

Tip: To crisp and char the Brussels sprouts, take them out of the foil and place directly on the grill for a couple of minutes, turning frequently.

❧ Peewee Potato Packs ❧
(TG or V)

Serves 4–6

Ingredients
25 to 30 peewee potatoes
1 garlic bulb
¼ cup olive oil
½ cup water
1 tablespoon dill or parsley, chopped
Pinch of coarse salt
Salt and pepper to taste
Heavy duty aluminum foil

Directions
Prepare grill for medium heat.

Cut off ¼- to ½-inch of the top of garlic cloves, exposing the individual cloves of garlic, and place in the middle of a large piece of heavy duty foil. Wash peewees, pat dry, and arrange around garlic bulb.

Make a pouch out of foil by bringing its sides up and together and drizzle its contents with olive oil. Sprinkle in salt. Pour in water and wrap the potatoes and garlic in the pouch.

Steam 25 to 45 minutes, depending on the grill's heat level. Check every 5 minutes by opening the foil and checking for tenderness. Add additional water if necessary.

When done, let the pouch rest for a few minutes, then squeeze the roasted garlic cloves out of their skins, mash with a fork, and spread over potatoes. Add more salt and pepper to taste. Sprinkle with chopped dill or parsley.

⋙ Vermont Maple Baked Beans with Bourbon ⋘
(DO)

Soak the beans overnight to give you a head start on this recipe when you get to the campground.

Serves 6

Ingredients

2 cups (1 pound) dried Great Northern beans, rinsed and picked over

1 tablespoon Dijon mustard

¼ teaspoon freshly ground pepper

¼ teaspoon ground ginger

1½ tablespoons cider vinegar

1½ cups strongly brewed coffee

½ cup grade B or dark amber maple syrup, or ½ cup grade A maple syrup plus 1 teaspoon molasses

1 medium onion, minced (about ⅔ cup)

¼ pound lean salt pork in one piece, with rind (omit if vegetarian)

¼ cup bourbon

Directions

> **Make ahead:** Soak beans in cold water to cover overnight or pour 2 quarts boiling water over beans in a heatproof large bowl and let stand 1 hour.

At the campsite: Prepare a fire and set up your Dutch oven tripod over fire. When fire is still very hot, drain beans in colander and transfer to Dutch oven. Add enough water to cover by 2 inches. Heat over high heat to boiling, then reduce heat and simmer, uncovered for 30 minutes or until beans are somewhat soft and swelled. Pour off all but 1½ cups of cooking liquid, reserving leftover liquid. Combine mustard, pepper, ginger, and vinegar in medium bowl. Stir in coffee and maple syrup. Pour over beans, and then add onion. Stir to combine. Score salt pork in crisscross pattern on fatty side without cutting through the rind. This helps fat melt more evenly and quickly without disintegrating. Place salt pork on beans rind side down. Place coals around base and top of Dutch oven to maintain a temperature of 300°F (see chart, page 23). Cook for 4 hours. Open lid and add bourbon. If beans seem dry, add ½ to 1 cup of reserved cooking liquid. Recover and cook an additional ½ to 1 hour. Interior of beans should be almost dry, although surface pools of liquid will appear as hot beans are spooned out of pot. These will be absorbed as beans stand.

⋙ Yvonne's Marinated Japanese Eggplants ⋘
(TG)

Marinate the eggplant at home and transport in your cooler to the campground.

Serves 4

Ingredients
4 Japanese eggplants
½ cup seasoned rice vinegar
½ cup soy sauce
1 tablespoon toasted dark sesame oil
1-inch piece fresh ginger, grated

Directions

Make ahead: For the marinade, combine all ingredients except the eggplant in a blender and mix. Place marinade in an airtight, leak-proof container. Slice eggplant lengthwise on a mandoline, ½ inch thick. Add to marinade, making sure all pieces are coated in marinade. Refrigerate until ready to transfer to cooler.

At the campsite: Prepare a fire. Let coals cool to medium heat. Place Tuscan grill over fire. Remove eggplant from the marinade and grill each piece 10 minutes per side. Serve warm or cold.

Tip: This eggplant would be a great appetizer, addition to a sandwich, or served as a side with our Beef and Pepper Skewers (page 124). You can also use them on our Veggie Skewers (page 155).

⤜ Zucchini with Shallots and Walnuts ⤛
(CS, TG, or V)

Serves 4

Ingredients
½ cup walnuts
2 garlic cloves, pressed
2 tablespoons fresh lemon juice
5 tablespoons olive oil
2 large shallots, chopped
1 pound zucchini, halved lengthwise
½ cup Italian parsley, coarsely chopped
Salt and pepper, to taste

Directions
Preheat grill for medium-high heat. Toast walnuts in a small skillet over medium heat on your camp stove, tossing often, about 5 minutes. Chop coarsely. Set aside. Add a little oil to the skillet and sauté shallots. Toss walnuts and shallots with garlic, lemon juice, and 3 tablespoons oil in a large bowl. Season with salt and pepper.

Brush zucchini with remaining oil, and season with salt and pepper. Grill, turning often, about 8 to 10 minutes. The zucchini should be al dente.

Cut zucchini into bite-size pieces and add to bowl with walnuts. Stir in parsley and toss to combine.

⇒ Cilantro Basmati Rice ⇐
(CS)

This is an easy-peasy recipe. Make the cilantro mixture ahead of time in your home blender, store in a container, and add to rice at the campsite.

Serves 4

Ingredients
1 cup basmati rice
Water
Cilantro Blend

Make ahead: Cilantro Blend

Directions
Puree the following ingredients in a blender and stir well into the rice once it is cooked.
⅔ cup cilantro, loosely packed
⅓ cup onion, chopped
¼ cup scallions, chopped
1 jalapeño (or to taste)
1 tablespoon lime juice
1 teaspoon olive oil

At the campsite: Cook rice according to package directions, using 1 teaspoon salt per cup of rice.

⋙ Dressed Up Brown Basmati Rice ⋘
(CS)

Serves 4

Ingredients
3 tablespoons butter
1 large onion, finely chopped
4 cloves garlic, minced
½ cup slivered almonds
1 cup brown basmati rice, rinsed well
½ cup raisins
½ teaspoon allspice, ground
1¼ teaspoons cinnamon
2 cups chicken stock
3 tablespoons fresh chopped parsley
Salt and pepper, to taste

Directions
Melt butter in skillet. Add onions, garlic, and almonds. Sauté 5 to 7 minutes until almonds and onions are golden. Add rice, raisins, allspice, and cinnamon, and sauté 2 minutes. Add stock and bring to a boil for 1 minute. Cover and reduce to simmer for 15 to 20 minutes. Add chopped fresh parsley, salt, and pepper. Stir with fork. Keep covered until serving time.

⇒ Farro with Greens and Sausage ⇐
(CS)

Make the farro ahead of time and dress it up at the campsite!

Serves 6–8

Ingredients

1 tablespoon olive oil
1 medium shallot, chopped
1 bunch of kale or chard, torn into medium-sized pieces
1 package fully cooked sausage, sliced (turkey, chicken, or other to your liking)

1 jar marinated artichokes
1 jar marinated mushrooms
1 package farro
Salt and pepper to taste

Directions

Make ahead: Cook farro according to package instructions. When cooled, place in a container and refrigerate until ready to transfer to your cooler.

At the campsite: In a medium pot, sauté chopped shallots in olive oil over medium-low heat until softened. Add greens and salt, cover for a few minutes until the greens start to soften. Remove lid and continue cooking until greens are done (they will darken in color). Remove greens and set aside.

Slice sausages, add them to the pan and cook until fully warmed and a bit brown. Add marinated artichokes and some of the oil they come in, along with the marinated mushrooms. Heat until warmed. Add greens back to the pot, and then add farro. Mix and serve.

⇒ Mediterranean Farro ⇐
(CS)

Here's a vegetarian option for cooking this ancient grain. Make the farro ahead of time.

Serves 8

Ingredients

2 cups farro
½ cup shelled pistachio nuts
1½ teaspoons finely grated lemon zest
3 tablespoons fresh lemon juice
1 teaspoon finely grated peeled ginger
½ teaspoon sugar
½ teaspoon kosher salt, plus more

⅓ cup olive oil
Freshly ground black pepper
1 serrano chile, sliced into rings (optional)
1 cup coarsely chopped fresh cilantro, mint, and parsley, mixed
⅓ cup golden raisins

Directions

Make ahead: Rinse farro under cold water. Cook in a large pot of boiling salted water, skimming surface occasionally, until tender, 20 to 25 minutes. Drain farro and rinse under cold water. When cooled, place in a container and refrigerate until ready to transfer to your cooler.

At the campsite: Toast pistachios in a small skillet over medium heat on your camp stove, tossing often, about 5 to 8 minutes. Chop coarsely. Set aside. In a medium bowl, whisk lemon zest, lemon juice, ginger, sugar, and ½ teaspoon salt together. Whisking constantly, gradually add oil. Whisk until emulsified. Season vinaigrette with salt and pepper. Transfer farro to a large bowl and add chile, herbs, raisins, and pistachios. Toss to combine. Drizzle with vinaigrette, season with salt and pepper, and toss to coat.

Harvest Grains with Hazelnuts (CS)

Trader Joe's carries this wonderful product called Harvest Grains Blend. It is made up of Israeli couscous, orzo, baby garbanzo beans, and red quinoa. Executive chef Denise tried it alone and found it a bit lacking in flavor, so she came up with the following recipe to make it worthy of the Gourmet Girls at Large!

Serves 4

Ingredients

½ package Harvest Grains (available at Trader Joe's)
1¾ cups water or chicken broth
2 tablespoons butter, separated
2 tablespoons olive oil
1 red bell pepper, diced small
1 leek, chopped
1 cup fresh mushrooms, chopped
2 cloves garlic, pressed
½ cup fresh parsley, chopped
½ cup shelled hazelnuts, chopped
Salt and pepper to taste

Directions

Cook harvest grains according to the instructions on the package. Set aside and keep warm. In a medium pan, sauté chopped leeks, garlic, bell pepper, and mushrooms in olive oil and butter over medium-low heat until softened.

Add all sautéed ingredients along with parsley and hazelnuts to harvest grains. Stir well to combine. Serve.

⋙ Mascarpone Polenta with Wild Mushrooms ⋘
(CS)

Serves 4

Ingredients

1½ cups polenta

5 cups water

Kosher salt

1 tablespoon unsalted butter

½ cup fresh or frozen sweet corn kernels

2 tablespoons mascarpone

White pepper

2 tablespoons extra virgin olive oil

1 small shallot, finely chopped

2 garlic cloves, finely sliced

5 cups thinly sliced mixed mushrooms (such as chanterelles, cremini, shiitake, beech, and oyster)

½ tablespoon finely chopped chives

½ tablespoon finely chopped flat-leaf parsley

2 tablespoons finely grated Parmesan

truffle oil (optional)

Salt and pepper to taste

Directions

In a large saucepot, bring 5 cups of salted water to a boil. Slowly add the polenta and whisk constantly until tender, about 7 to 10 minutes. Use a wooden spoon to stir in the butter, corn, and mascarpone. Season with salt and white pepper. Set aside.

In a large skillet set over medium heat, warm the olive oil. Add the shallot and garlic and cook until translucent. Add the mushrooms and cook until they soften slightly, about 7 to 10 minutes. Stir herbs into the polenta and spread the polenta on a serving platter. Spoon the mushrooms onto the center of the polenta and drizzle lightly with optional truffle oil. Sprinkle with the Parmesan and serve immediately.

Tip: This dish is sublime as a base for our Grilled Rack of Lamb recipe (page 132). Just place a dollop on a plate and then place two or three ribs of lamb on top. Add Maple-Roasted Brussels Sprouts on the Grill (page 174) or Haricots Verts with Shiitake Mushrooms and Pine Nuts (page 173), and voila! Yum!

⋙ Quinoa with Cauliflower and Walnuts ⋘
(CS)

This recipe courtesy of Bon Appétit.

Serves 6

Ingredients
½ cup red or white quinoa
½ head of cauliflower, coarsely grated
½ cup finely chopped parsley, plus some leaves for garnish
½ cup roughly chopped, pitted Kalamata olives
⅓ cup olive oil
⅓ cup toasted chopped walnuts
2 tablespoons lemon juice, plus more
1 teaspoon lemon zest
½ teaspoon ground cumin
Salt and pepper to taste

Directions
Bring a large pot of salted water to a boil. Add quinoa and simmer until fully cooked, about 15 minutes. Drain and return quinoa to pot. Cover with a lid and let it sit for 5 additional minutes. Fluff with a fork and transfer to a large bowl or sheet pan to cool. Combine cooled quinoa and the remaining ingredients in a large bowl. Season with salt, pepper, and more lemon juice, if desired. Transfer to a large serving bowl or platter, and scatter parsley leaves over. Serve cold or room temperature.

Getting Sauced and Buttered Up

Don't let a bland meal get the best of you. Throw one of these sauces together and watch that salmon go from bland to blammo!

The first time we tried the dill sauce called for in the Campfire Salmon with Lemon Dill Cream Sauce recipe (Campfire Salmon, page 96; Lemon Dill Cream Sauce, page 194) we thought all was lost. The sauce had thinned out between cooking it at home, being refrigerated, and then reheated at the campsite. Luckily executive chef Denise, always the expert in these matters, came to the rescue. If your sauce thins out, turn up the heat for a minute to boil off excess water. Reconstitute any separation with a bit of butter once you've taken it off the heat. Most sauces can be precooked up to a certain point and only require minimal finishing on site.

One of our all time favorites is the Blender Hollandaise (page 189). This fantastic make-ahead sauce stores extremely well and is super versatile. It's normally the star of our eggs Benedict morning show, but we also love it poured over grilled asparagus or used as a dipping sauce for pretty much anything you can dream up.

⋐ Béarnaise Butter ⋑

Serves 4

Ingredients
3 tablespoons unsalted butter, softened
2 teaspoons finely chopped fresh tarragon leaves
2 teaspoons minced shallot
½ teaspoon fresh lemon juice
⅛ teaspoon salt

Directions
In a small bowl, blend all ingredients together well with a fork and transfer to a sheet of wax paper. Using wax paper or plastic wrap as an aid, shape butter into a 4-inch long log and wrap. Chill butter 1 hour or until firm. Béarnaise butter may be made 5 days ahead and kept chilled, wrapped tightly, until ready to transfer to cooler. It can also be frozen.

Tip: Try this Béarnaise Butter on our grilled corn on the cob or on a fish fillet. Delicious!

⋐ Béarnaise Sauce ⋑
(CS)

Makes ¾ cup

Ingredients
2 tablespoons dry white wine
2 tablespoons tarragon vinegar
1 tablespoon shallot, minced
½ teaspoon fresh tarragon leaves, chopped and reserved
4 whole black peppercorns, lightly crushed
Blender Hollandaise (page 189), made with water instead of lemon juice

Directions
Combine all ingredients except hollandaise and tarragon leaves in a small saucepan. Bring to a simmer, uncovered, until reduced to 1 tablespoon. Strain through a fine mesh sieve and let cool. Stir the liquid into blender hollandaise. Stir in minced tarragon leaves. Let cool, then place in airtight container and refrigerate until ready to transfer to cooler. Reheat slowly in a stainless steel bowl set over hot water, whisking constantly. Serve immediately.

⮞ Blender Hollandaise ⮜

Unless you've got the power to run a blender in the wilderness, this is a definite make-ahead for your camping trips! Pictured on page 186.

Serves 4

Ingredients
1 whole cube unsalted butter, melted
Juice of ½ lemon
Pinch of cayenne
3 egg yolks

Directions
Melt butter, add lemon juice and cayenne, and place in a measuring cup. Place 3 egg yolks in a blender, turn it on, and slowly drip in melted butter mixture. The sauce should begin to thicken immediately. When emulsified, turn off blender and let cool. Transfer hollandaise into a tightly sealed container or a resealable bag. Refrigerate until ready to transfer to cooler.

Tip: The hollandaise sauce is great over asparagus too!

⮞ Chimichurri Sauce ⮜

This is a marvelous, spicy hot Argentinian sauce, served with grilled or roasted meat.

Makes 1¼ cups

Ingredients
½ cup olive oil
¼ cup red wine vinegar
1 small onion, finely chopped
½ cup packed fresh cilantro leaves, chopped
4 garlic cloves, finely chopped
1 tablespoon finely chopped oregano
1 teaspoon salt
¼ teaspoon ground red pepper, or to taste
¼ teaspoon black pepper, or to taste

Directions
Whisk together olive oil and red wine vinegar thoroughly in a small bowl. Stir in remaining ingredients. Cover and let stand for 2 to 3 hours to allow the flavors to develop. The sauce will keep, covered and refrigerated, for 2 days. Bring to forest temperature before using.

⋙ Cilantro Pesto ⋘

This recipe is courtesy of Modern Mexican Flavors *by Richard Sandoval.*

Makes ¾ cup

Ingredients

1 tablespoon canola oil, plus ¼ cup
½ cup chopped white Spanish onion
½ cup packed fresh cilantro leaves, chopped
½ cup packed fresh snipped chives
¼ cup pine nuts, toasted
1 fresh serrano chile, stemmed, seeded and chopped
1 teaspoon roasted garlic puree (or more, to taste)

1 tablespoon sherry wine vinegar
2 teaspoons freshly squeezed lemon juice
1 to 2 teaspoons of honey
½ teaspoon salt
⅛ teaspoon white pepper
1 tablespoon Cotija cheese or Parmesan cheese (or more, to taste)
¼ cup olive oil

Directions

In a small skillet, heat the 1 tablespoon of canola oil over medium-high heat. Add the onion and sauté until tender and browned, 3 to 4 minutes. Scrape into a blender. To the blender add the cilantro, chives, pines nuts, chile, roasted garlic puree, sherry wine vinegar, lemon juice, honey, salt, white pepper, and cheese. Blend until pureed. Mix together ¼ cup canola oil and ¼ cup olive oil in a measuring cup. With the blender running, gradually add the oil in a thin stream until well blended. Store, tightly covered, in the refrigerator. Transfer to cooler when packing up for camping.

Tip: This pesto is great on shrimp and as an accompaniment to most seafood.

⮞ Cinnamon Rum Sauce ⮜

Serves 6–8

Ingredients
1 cup sugar
½ cup butter
2 tablespoons flour
1 cup hot water
1 teaspoon cinnamon
½ teaspoon rum flavoring

Directions
Cook first 4 ingredients in saucepan over medium-high heat, stirring occasionally, 6 to 8 minutes until thickened. Stir in cinnamon and rum flavoring.

⮞ Cucumber Yogurt Raita ⮜

Serves 8

Ingredients
1 cup plain low-fat yogurt
¾ cup chopped English cucumber
1 teaspoon minced fresh ginger
1 teaspoon minced garlic
Salt

Directions
In a small bowl, mix yogurt, cucumber, ginger, garlic, and salt to taste.

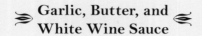

Garlic, Butter, and White Wine Sauce

Serves 2

Ingredients
2 tablespoons unsalted butter
2 cloves garlic, chopped
1 cup white wine
1 teaspoon Pernod
1 tablespoon heavy cream
1 tablespoon chopped fresh dill
Dash of salt

Directions
Sauté garlic in butter for 1 to 2 minutes. Add wine and Pernod. Bring to a boil, then add cream and salt. Lower heat to medium-low and reduce sauce to ½ cup. Sauce should be thick enough to thinly coat the back of a spoon. Remove from heat and stir in fresh dill.

Horseradish Butter

Makes enough for 24 oysters

Ingredients
1 pound unsalted butter, at room temperature
½ cup prepared horseradish
Zest of ½ lemon
2 teaspoons kosher salt
1½ cups grated Parmesan cheese
1 tablespoon chopped chives

Directions
Using a spatula, combine butter, horseradish, lemon zest, and salt in a medium bowl. After oysters begin to open on the grill, shuck each one and place the oysters aside in a small bowl. Put 1 tablespoon of horseradish butter in each bottom shell. Top the butter with 1 oyster per shell. Cover each oyster with 1 tablespoon of Parmesan cheese. Place oysters back on the grill until cheese is melted and butter is bubbling. Garnish each oyster with chives before serving.

Harissa Mayonnaise

Makes ¾ cup

Ingredients
½ cup mayonnaise
¼ cup sour cream
2 tablespoons harissa paste
½ teaspoon red wine vinegar
¼ teaspoon ground cumin
Salt and freshly cracked black pepper

Directions
Mix the mayonnaise, sour cream, harissa, vinegar, and cumin together in a large bowl and stir with a whisk to combine. Taste for seasoning and add salt and pepper, to taste. Refrigerate and serve smeared on spice lamb burgers.

Variation: Mix one cup of jar mayonnaise with a teaspoon of caraway seeds and 2 tablespoons harissa; season with salt and pepper.

Homemade Rosemary Garlic Mayonnaise

Makes ¾ cup

Ingredients
1 egg yolk
2 teaspoons lemon juice, freshly squeezed
1 teaspoon coarse-ground or Dijon mustard
½ cup canola oil
¼ cup olive oil
2 small cloves garlic, pressed
1 teaspoon fresh rosemary, chopped
¼ heaping teaspoon kosher salt
⅛ teaspoon freshly ground black pepper

Directions
In medium bowl, whisk egg, lemon, and mustard. Combine oils in separate container and, while whisking the egg mixture vigorously, add a few drops of the oil mixture. When they are completely combined, add a little more oil until you're adding it in a steady stream. Continue whisking vigorously for 30-60 seconds or until thickened. Add garlic and rosemary. Then add salt and pepper to taste. Place in cooler for at least an hour before serving. This will keep for up to 3 to 5 days.

Tip: You can also take 1 cup store bought mayo, add ¼ cup minced rosemary and pressed garlic to taste. Stir well.

⇒ Jajik ⇐

Makes 2½ cups

Ingredients
2 cups Greek yogurt
2 to 3 garlic cloves, crushed
2 medium peeled cucumbers, diced
2 tablespoons fresh mint, chopped
2 tablespoons olive oil
½ teaspoon salt

Directions
Combine all ingredients in a serving bowl. Refrigerate at least 1 hour or overnight for flavors to mingle. When ready to serve, stir to combine.

Tip: Jajik can also be served as a dip with pita chips or vegetable crudité.

⇒ Lemon Dill Cream Sauce ⇐ (CS)

This sauce can be made ahead, stored in an airtight container, and refrigerated until ready to transfer to cooler. To reheat at the campsite over camp stove, place sauce in a saucepan and heat up over very low heat.

Makes 1¼ cups

Ingredients
2 cloves garlic, minced
½ cup dry white wine or chicken stock
2 tablespoons lemon juice
3 tablespoons fresh dill, chopped
½ teaspoon Dijon mustard
½ cup heavy cream
3 tablespoons unsalted butter, divided
Pinch cayenne pepper
½ teaspoon salt
½ teaspoon fresh ground black pepper

Directions
Add garlic, wine or chicken stock, lemon juice, and dill to a small saucepan over medium heat. Bring to a boil and boil for about 2 minutes. Reduce heat and whisk in mustard and heavy cream. Continue to cook until it thickens, making sure to whisk the entire time. Remove from heat and whisk in butter pieces one at a time. Add cayenne pepper, salt, and pepper.

⤜ Lemon-Cayenne Vin Blanc ⤛ (CS)

Enough for 24 oysters

Ingredients
1 cup dry white wine
1 small shallot, minced
1¼ cups water
¼ cup heavy cream
2 teaspoons instant fish bouillon
3 tablespoons salted butter
3 tablespoons all-purpose flour
½ teaspoon cayenne pepper
2 tablespoons fresh lemon juice

Directions
Combine wine and shallots in a saucepan and bring to a boil. Cook until reduced by half, about 15 minutes. Add water, cream, and bouillon; bring to a boil. Melt butter in saucepan over medium heat. Add flour and stir, until it smells toasty, about 1 minute. Don't let flour brown. Add half the wine mixture and stir well to dissolve the roux. Stir in remaining liquid and bring to a simmer. Add cayenne pepper, reduce heat to low, and simmer, stirring constantly for 5 minutes. Stir in lemon juice. Strain sauce through a fine-mesh strainer. Using a knife, sever the muscle on the shell of each partly opened oyster. Discard the top shells. Spoon 2 teaspoons of sauce on each oyster, set on a hot grill, cook until the edges of the oysters start to ruffle and sauce starts to sizzle.

⤜ Mango-Peach Salsa ⤛

Makes 1¾ cups

Ingredients
1½ cups coarsely chopped ripe mango
1 fresh ripe peach, skinned and coarsely chopped
2 fresh jalapeños, seeded and minced
1 clove garlic, minced
3 tablespoons finely chopped red onion
3 tablespoons chopped cilantro
3 tablespoons chopped parsley
3 to 4 tablespoons freshly squeezed lime juice
2 tablespoons olive oil
Salt and pepper to tasted

Directions
Combine all ingredients in an airtight container and refrigerate until ready to transfer to your cooler. Makes about 2 cups.

❧ Red Wine Reduction Sauce ❧
(CS)

Makes 1½ cups

Ingredients
2 tablespoons butter
1 large shallot, minced
1 clove garlic, pressed
1 tablespoons fresh thyme leaves
½ cup chopped button mushrooms
1½ cups dry red wine
1 cup beef broth
2 tablespoons heavy cream
Salt and pepper to taste

Directions
In a medium sauté pan over medium heat, melt the butter and sauté the chopped shallot until slightly browned. Add the garlic, thyme, and mushrooms and sauté for 5 minutes, then add the wine and broth. Cook the mixture until it has reduced to 1 cup, then add the cream. Sauce is done when bubbles are evenly distributed across the surface of the sauce. It should be thickened enough to coat the back of a spoon.

❧ Romesco Sauce ❧
(CS)

Makes ¾ cup

Ingredients
2 tablespoons blanched almonds, roughly chopped
1 garlic cloves, pressed
¼ cup organic mayonnaise
1 tablespoon sherry wine vinegar
2 roasted red peppers or jarred piquillo peppers, finely chopped

Directions
Toast almonds in a small pan and place in a bowl. Mix together mayonnaise, sherry vinegar, piquillo peppers, half the pressed garlic and a splash of olive oil. Add to the almonds. Stir until combined. Season with salt and pepper.

Tip: Romesco sauce would be good over eggplant, cauliflower, or any kind of squash.

⇒ Smoky Tomato Sauce ⇐

Makes ¾ cup

Ingredients
2 small ripe tomatoes (about ½ pound)
3 anchovy fillets packed in oil, drained, finely chopped
1 small garlic clove, finely chopped
1 teaspoon harissa paste
1 teaspoon red wine vinegar
2 tablespoons extra virgin olive oil plus more for serving
Kosher salt
Freshly ground pepper
Chopped fresh flat-leaf parsley and lemon wedges (for serving)

Directions
Grill tomatoes, turning occasionally, until skins are blackened and split, about 4 minutes. Press through a sieve over a medium bowl, discard solids. Whisk in anchovies, garlic, harissa, vinegar, and 2 tablespoons oil. Season with salt and pepper.

Tip: This sauce can be made ahead at the campsite. Cover and chill.

⇒ Yogurt and Sumac Sauce ⇐

Makes 1¼ cups

Ingredients
1 small garlic clove, finely chopped
1 cup plain Greek yogurt
2 tablespoons extra virgin olive oil plus more for serving
½ teaspoon sumac plus more for serving
Kosher salt

Directions
Whisk garlic, yogurt, 2 tablespoons oil, and ½ teaspoon sumac in a medium bowl. Season with salt.

Tip: Can be made ahead at the campsite. Cover and chill.

Divine Desserts

Some people are born with a sweet tooth. Then there are those aliens who nobody understands. We recommend Maryann's Campfire Cobbler recipe (page 204) for the humans, and a plate of fruit and cheese for the aliens. All joking aside, these desserts have been carefully tested to include the perfect amount of sweetness to satisfy terrestrial as well as nonterrestrial campers. Just remember to bring your toothbrush with you on that final trip to the bathroom. There's nothing worse than getting all the way up there and having to come to grips with the fact that you're too lazy to go back and get it. You will just have to live with fuzzy peach cobbler teeth until morning. Oh, the shame!

There was much debate as to whether or not to include a recipe for s'mores. As you'll see we couldn't in good conscience make a camping cookbook without covering the flaming hot topic of s'mores. Hopefully you'll have as much fun trying to get the melted chocolate out of your camping chair as we did! Here's a little hint: it's going to be there forever. A tiny brown reminder of all the fun you had while attempting to melt chocolate using nothing but a fiery hot marshmallow and your dirty little camp fingers. May the best camper win.

⮞ Easy Strawberry Shortcake ⮜
(CS)

Serves 4

Ingredients
2 pints organic strawberries, sliced (reserve 4 whole berries for garnish)
¼ cup sugar
Juice from ½ lemon
Juice from 1 orange
Zest from 1 lemon
1 Sara Lee Pound Cake (found in the freezer section of your grocery store)
Whipping cream

Directions
Combine 2 pints strawberries, sugar, citrus juice, and zest together in a bowl. Stir to combine. Cut pound cake in ½-inch thick slices, two per person, then using an empty can or a 2½-inch round cookie cutter, cut out circles from the center of the pound cake slices. Place a pound cake round on a plate, top with a swirl of whipped cream, add berry mixture, and then whipped cream. Top that with another round of pound cake, berries, and cream. Pour ¼ cup strawberry sauce on plate around cake, and drizzle a little over top of cream. Garnish with a mint leaf and a whole strawberry. Serve.

Strawberry Sauce

Ingredients
1 pint organic strawberries
¼ cup sugar
⅛ teaspoon salt
1 tablespoon lemon juice
2 tablespoons raspberry liqueur (available at Trader Joe's)

Directions

Stir together berries, sugar, salt, lemon juice, and raspberry liqueur in a saucepan. Bring to a boil, mashing with a potato masher and stirring frequently. Cook at a low boil stirring more frequently as mixture thickens, until sauce clings to a spoon, about 10 minutes. Skim foam from top. Let cool completely. Strain through a sieve.

Tip: Use other fruit combinations with the strawberries like blackberries, peaches etc.

⋙ Lemon Ricotta Crepes ⋘
(CS)

Since many of you may not have the time to make crepes from scratch, purchase Frieda's French Style Crêpes at your local market. They are quite good and work really well in this recipe. Photo page 198.

Serves 6

Ingredients
1 package of Frieda's French Style Crêpes (widely available in grocery stores)

Garnish
½ cup water
1 thinly sliced lemon
½ cup sugar

Filling
½ teaspoon finely grated lemon zest
2 teaspoons lemon juice
1 cup ricotta cheese

1 tablespoon honey, plus more for serving
Handful of blackberries
Mint leaves

Directions
On your camp stove, in a medium saucepan, boil ½ cup of water and ½ cup of sugar, stirring, until the sugar dissolves. Add the lemon slices and simmer until tender and translucent, 5 to 7 minutes. Remove the lemon slices and set aside. Continue to cook the remaining liquid until it becomes syrupy, about 5 minutes more.

In a small bowl, combine the lemon zest, lemon juice, ricotta, and honey. Lay out the individual crepes and dividing evenly, spread the ricotta mixture on the crepes (about 2 tablespoons each), and roll up. Place on a plate, seam side down. Drizzle with additional honey and reduced lemon-sugar syrup. Serve topped with the lemon slices and blackberries. Garnish with mint leaves.

⋗ Lyn's Persimmon Pudding ⋖
(DO)

A great make-ahead dessert to bring to camp or bake it in your Dutch oven at the campsite!
Even the Cinnamon Rum Sauce (page 191) can be made at home since it stores, travels, and reheats well.

Serves 6-8

Ingredients
2 cups persimmon pulp, mashed (We use a potato masher.)
½ cup butter
1 cup sugar
2 large eggs
1 cup flour
1½ teaspoons baking powder
½ teaspoon baking soda
1 teaspoon cinnamon
½ cup milk
½ cup buttermilk, or regular milk

Directions
Prepare a coal fire for Dutch oven cooking at 350°F. In a large bowl, stir together first 4 ingredients until blended. Add flour and next 5 ingredients, stirring well. Batter will not be smooth. Pour batter into parchment-lined Dutch oven.

Bake at 350°F for 55 minutes.

Serve with Cinnamon Rum Sauce (page 191). Whip up fresh cream lightly sweetened for the top to make an extra yummy and sinful dessert.

⪜ Maryann's Campfire Cobbler ⪜ (DO)

This recipe is for a 12-inch Dutch oven.

Serves 6–8

Ingredients
2½ to 3 pounds seasonal fruit (peaches, blueberries, and blackberries, etc.)
2 tablespoons rye whiskey (optional)
1 box yellow cake mix
6 ounces of a natural soda with pure cane sugar (ginger or flower-flavored soda like a lavender or rose petal, if you can find it)
3 tablespoons tapioca
Whipped cream (optional)

Directions
Prepare a coal fire for Dutch oven cooking at 300°F (see chart, page 23). Line Dutch oven with parchment. Delicately combine fruit and whiskey, if using, in the Dutch oven.

Empty cake mix into bowl and combine with natural soda and tapioca. It will be lumpy. Pour batter over fruit filling. Cover Dutch oven with lid and arrange 6-10 hot coals under oven in firepit. Add 10 to 12 coals on top of lid.

Bake for 30 to 35 minutes, until top is golden and filling is bubbling. Let cool 10 minutes. Top with whipped cream.

Tip: During the baking process, you can check the cake consistency with a toothpick or bamboo skewer, but be careful not to let any ash fall into the Dutch oven!

⇒ Maryann's Campfire Orange Bombs ⇐

Serves 6

Ingredients
6 large oranges with thick skin,
Sumos if you can find them
1 box brownie or chocolate cake mix
Almond extract or amaretto (optional)
Egg
Oil
Water
Marshmallows (optional)

Directions
Cut top third of oranges off. These will be the caps. Scoop out the orange flesh in the orange rind caps and set aside. Use a knife to gently loosen the orange flesh from the bottom two-thirds of the oranges, keeping the shells intact. Use a spoon to scoop out the orange flesh as much as you can. These will be the cups.

Mix the batter according to box directions. Fill orange cup bottoms with batter about an inch from the rim. Cover orange cups with rind caps. Securely wrap each orange bomb in foil.

Place all bombs, cap up, into the firepit over coals. Rotate the bombs after 20 to 25 minutes, carefully turning them on their sides. After 5 to 10 minutes more, check one of the bomb cake's consistency with a toothpick. If it comes out clean, your bombs are done. If not, cover back up and place in firepit for another 5 to 10 minutes. Be careful not to overcook.

Carefully unwrap foil and remove caps (bombs are super hot). Top with a fire-roasted marshmallow, if desired. Enjoy with a spoon right out of the orange!

⋙ Outdoor Chocolate Fondue ⋘
(CS)

Serves 4–6

Ingredients
8 ounces heavy cream
12 ounces of Toblerone chocolate, cut into triangles
A pinch of salt
Kahlua (optional)
Dippables such as bananas, strawberries, apple slices, dried apricots, pear, etc. The sky's the limit!

Directions
In a saucepan, warm the cream over moderate heat until tiny bubbles show and begin to slowly boil. Add the chocolate and whisk until smooth. The trick here is to melt the chocolate slowly, then add optional liqueur. Keep the chocolate mixture warm over the Tuscan grill, away from direct heat.

Dip your choice of fruit in chocolate and gobble up!

Variation: Because you're outdoors, you should have some graham crackers and marshmallows to dip in there as well for fondue-style s'mores!

⋙ S'mores Ideas from Wendy ⋘

Here are a couple of new spins on this campfire delight from longtime Gourmet Girl Wendy Overend.

Ginger Snap S'mores

Use two ginger snaps (we recommend Trader Joe's gluten free) to sandwich the baked toasted marshmallow. Be sure to squeeze in a piece of Terry's Chocolate Orange or a dark chocolate orange stick or two. The easy path is to use two Pim's Orange Biscuits to sandwich the toasted marshmallow.

Minty S'mores

Another way to create a fresh take on the s'mores is to use a mint chocolate. I've used Frango Mint Chocolates, York Peppermint Patties, Andes Chocolate Mints, After Eight Chocolate Thins, etc. All make for a surprising kick and delectable fireside dessert. Stuff the mint chocolate into the melted marshmallow and squeeze between two soft madeleines rather than the standard graham cracker.

The Neurotic Woodsman*

Some people might tell you there is no right way to camp. These people are wrong. A tidy campsite is a happy campsite. At the Neurotic Woodsman's campsite, there will be no tripping over empty fuel canisters or strewn beer bottles. No searching for dirty tongs in a pile of last night's dishes. After each of your fabulous meals, clean the (bad word my editor wouldn't let me say) up.

However, while the Neurotic Woodsman does run a tight ship, he also knows when it's time to relax. It's fine to leave dishes until the morning because your afternoon cocktail hour may have lasted until midnight, but for heaven's sake, leave them soaking in a bin of warm soapy water. Sure, beer bottles and other recyclables will accumulate. Designate an area as the bottle graveyard so no one breaks an ankle on the way to the bathroom. Follow these simple rules and your campsite will pass an inspection from the Neurotic Woodsman, and the massive bear lurking just behind that tree on your left.

*Of course when we say woodsman, we mean woodswoman. It just doesn't roll off the tongue as well, and spell check is telling me that it's not an actual word.

Acknowledgments

First we want to thank the wonderful women who we've been cooking with for the last twenty years. The inspiration for the book itself. The Gourmet Girls at Large: Lyn Burich, Yvonne Chin, Maury Treman, Wendy Overend, Jen Shively, and Seyburn Zorthian. It is because of your love and support all these years that this book is even remotely possible. From the bottom of our hearts, thank you.

To Adam James, our fabulous photographer and videographer whose brilliance shines through in every beautiful picture.

To TJ Moran, for listening, repeatedly.

To Kathy Moran, for creating one of the most beautiful and professional websites we've ever laid eyes on. Your patience is greatly appreciated.

To Lorna Johnson, for answering our many, many novice questions about book design and printing.

To Joni Wilson, for her eagle eye in proofreading the layout.

To Maryann Feierstein and Arny Cano, for contributing some truly unique and delicious recipes, being awesome camping compadres, and allowing us to use a few fabulous photos from camping excursions in years past.

A special thanks to Seyburn Zorthian for her unwavering support and generosity.

We've all spent many long hours in the kitchen, at the campground, and at the computer to make this book a reality. Quite a different experience from lounging around the campfire where the idea was conceived. Regardless, having the finished product is a feeling unlike any other. It took a lot of people to get us to this point and just because your name isn't listed here does not mean we don't appreciate those close to us who sat and listened when we needed it most.

Thank you,

Gail M. Kearns   Denise J. Woolery